The Planning of
Industrial Investment Programs
A Methodology

A WORLD BANK RESEARCH PUBLICATION

Volume One of
THE PLANNING OF INVESTMENT PROGRAMS
Alexander Meeraus and Ardy J. Stoutjesdijk, Editors

David A. Kendrick
Ardy J. Stoutjesdijk

The Planning of
Industrial Investment
Programs

A Methodology

Published for the World Bank
THE JOHNS HOPKINS UNIVERSITY PRESS
Baltimore and London

Library of Congress Cataloging in Publication Data
Kendrick, David A
  The planning of industrial investment programs.

  (The Planning of investment programs; v. 1)
  Includes bibliographies and index.
  1.   Industrial project management—Mathematical
models.   2.   Economic development projects—Evaluation—
Mathematical models.   I.   Stoutjesdijk, Ardy J., 1938–
joint author.   II.   Title.   III.   Series.
HD69.P75K46   658.4'04   78-8428
ISBN 0-8018-2139-8
ISBN 0-8018-2152-5 pbk.

Contents

Introduction to the Series *by Hollis B. Chenery*   *ix*

Editors' Note to the Series   *xi*

Preface   *xiii*

1. Introduction   *1*

The Difficulty of Planning Investment Programs *3*
The Apparent Ease of Project Planning
   in Some Circumstances *4*
A Systematic Approach to Project Planning
   under Economies of Scale *6*
The Criterion for Project Selection *9*
Previous Work on Project Planning
   under Economies of Scale *11*
A Reader's Guide to the Volume *14*

2. A Description of the Model   *16*

A Transport Model *16*
Bringing Production Cost into the Model *17*
A Process Model *18*
A Project Selection Model *21*

3. Mathematical Development of the Model   *23*

A Transport Model *23*
Bringing Production Cost into the Model *26*
A Multiproduct Model *27*

A Process Model *29*
Interplant Shipments, Exports, and Imports *33*
A Multiperiod Model with Investment *38*
Two Further Modifications *45*
Appendix. The Capital Recovery Factor *47*

4. A Model for Project Selection   *50*

The Complete Model *51*
Size of the Model *55*
Variants of the Model *58*
The LEGO Set *61*

5. Data   *63*

Set Specification *63*
Demand *67*
Supply *69*
Prices and Costs *72*
Other Data for the Complete Model *77*
Data Requirements for Variants
   of the Complete Model *78*

6. Uses of the Model   *81*

Determination of Efficient Shipping Patterns *82*
Project and Program Selection *83*
Economic Integration Studies *85*
Export Analysis *86*
Regulation *88*
Concluding Remarks *89*

7. Limitations of the Model   *90*

The Objective Function and Fixed Demands *91*
No Substitution in Demand *98*
Prices of Some Inputs and Outputs Fixed *99*
No Uncertainty *100*
Representation of Policy Objectives *100*
Size of the Programming Problem *101*
Conclusion *101*

8. Solution Methods   *103*

General-Purpose Computer Codes *104*
Hand Calculations *110*
Alternative Solutions *123*
Conclusion *123*

9. Summary and Conclusions   *125*

Index   *129*

Text Figures

1. Shipments from Plants to Markets *18*
2. The Investment Cost Function *39*
3. Investment Cost Function with Diseconomies of Scale *43*
4. A Piecewise Linear Approximation to an Investment
   Cost Function with Diseconomies of Scale *44*
5. The Consumers' and Producers' Surplus *93*
6. A Piecewise Linear Approximation to the Area
   under the Demand Curve *95*
7. The Binary Tree *106*
8. The Method of Branch and Bound *108*
9. The Demand Specification for the Calculation
   of Excess Capacity *117*

Text Tables

1. Typical Values for Capital Recovery Factors *49*
2. Domestic Production Compared with Imports:
   Some Hypothetical Data *112*
3. Typical Values for $1/[(1 + \rho)^n - 1]$ *118*

Introduction to the Series

AMONG THE FIRST RESEARCH PROJECTS launched by the World Bank Development Research Center in the early seventies was one addressed to the question "Does interdependence matter?" To answer this question, several studies have analyzed the significance for investment planning of interdependence among economic activities, with reference to particular industrial sectors. These include the fertilizer industry, mechanical engineering, and the production of heavy electrical equipment.

The first results of this research, which was undertaken both at a theoretical level and at a highly disaggregated empirical level, are to be published under the title *Industrial Investment Analysis under Increasing Returns*, edited by Ardy Stoutjesdijk and Larry E. Westphal. Two main conclusions emerged from that study. First, in the presence of significant economies of scale, interdependence is important enough to warrant explicit recognition in the investment planning phase. Second, computer technology has progressed so far that combinatorial problems that took many hours to solve only a decade ago can now be handled within a few minutes. This permits a far more comprehensive and systematic analysis of sectorwide investment planning problems than was possible hitherto.

Such technological advances are revolutionizing the analysis of investment projects. Until recently, it was a time-consuming task to compute the economic and financial implications of even a small number of variants of a given investment possibility. The literature on project evaluation has therefore focused on the rate of return for a single variant of an investment project, dismissing others according to fairly arbitrary decision rules. The use of mathematical programming and modern computers now enables the project analyst to examine many variants of a given project or groups of interdependent projects.

To make this methodology available to a wider audience, several volumes will be issued on the application of mathematical programming to the design and evaluation of investment programs. This introductory volume outlines the properties of such models and assesses their applicability to various types of problems. It therefore provides a background for the subsequent studies of individual sectors, and it also draws on their conclusions.

Although this series is addressed primarily to the practical planner, we hope that it may also be of interest to students of development economics and planning.

HOLLIS B. CHENERY
Vice President
Development Policy Staff
The World Bank

Washington, D.C.
June 1978

Editors' Note to the Series

THIS IS THE FIRST IN A SERIES of volumes dealing with the use of mathematical programming methods in investment analysis. This volume is designed to introduce students and project analysts to the use and properties of these methods. It will be followed by separate, self-contained volumes on specific industrial sectors and subsectors. These volumes contain a detailed description of an application of the methodology. Another volume in the series will deal with the specific problems that arise in the case of integration project planning within a common market. Finally, a Users' Guide will focus in more detail on the practical use of the methods proposed. In all the volumes, no knowledge of mathematical programming or computer algorithms is assumed, and the material is developed fully in steps of slowly increasing complexity.

The series relies essentially on one among a number of possible approaches to investment planning; specifically, it employs mixed-integer programming to analyze investment problems in the presence of economies of scale. Alternative approaches, such as dynamic programming, are successfully used to address selected aspects of the investment planning problem by other investigators. For sectorwide investment analysis, however, we considered that mixed-integer programming offered the best prospects for operational use.

ALEXANDER MEERAUS
ARDY STOUTJESDIJK

Washington, D.C.
June 1978

Preface

THE DESIGN OF AN INVESTMENT PROGRAM within the industrial sector normally faces three types of difficulties. First, a large number of project or program variants are possible in terms of timing, scale, location, technology, and product mixes. Second, many industrial activities exhibit economies of scale, that is, increasing returns on investment as total capacity increases. Third, the sector is characterized by strong interdependencies among activities. These characteristics of the sector have caused many economic planners to be considerably dissatisfied with the state of the art in industrial project identification.

Once a representation of an interdependent set of industrial activities is formulated, the computer can be used efficiently to investigate the economic properties of large numbers of alternative designs of investment programs. Essentially, this means that for the process industries—industries that use and produce fairly homogeneous products—a more systematic approach to investment programming is possible. Industries such as cement, steel, fertilizer, and pulp and paper lend themselves well to this treatment. In contrast, the non-process industries, such as the mechanical engineering industries, are much more difficult to capture in the form of a manageable model because of the extreme variety in products and equipment; only sporadically have attempts been made to systematize planning for such activities. The methods proposed in this volume focus primarily on designing investment programs in the process industries.

A model for the planning of industrial investment programs is developed, and guidelines for its use are set out. This model permits decisions about size, location, time-phasing, technology, and product mix to be made within its framework. Also, an example is given of how the analyst can reduce the model in order to let only size or time-phasing vary while holding location and technology fixed.

We are grateful to Bela Balassa, Hans Bergendorff, David Caplin, John H. Duloy, Benjamin B. King, Alexander Meeraus, Roger Norton, D. C. Rao, and J. Scott Rogers for comments and suggestions. The final manuscript was edited by Robert Faherty.

DAVID KENDRICK
University of Texas at Austin

ARDY STOUTJESDIJK
Development Economics Department
The World Bank

The Planning of
Industrial Investment Programs

A Methodology

1

Introduction

PROJECT EVALUATION occupies an important place in the economic literature. The Organization for Economic Cooperation and Development (OECD) and the United Nations Industrial Development Organization (UNIDO) have sponsored recent manuals on project evaluation, usually referred to as the OECD Manual[1] and the UNIDO Manual.[2] With the publication of these manuals, new impetus was given to the debate on the relative merits of various techniques of project evaluation, no doubt leading to further refinements in the measurement of the impact of projects on a variety of objectives.

The emphasis on the appropriate definition and measurement of costs and benefits of a given project, however, appears to have diverted attention away from the more basic problem of project planning, that is, how to select, formulate, and design a project in the first place. Both manuals exclude the problem of project planning from the start, and they make only slight references to the need for ranking all possible projects and for evaluating sets of interdependent projects rather than projects in isolation. The OECD Manual is most explicit in this respect: "From now on, since our subject is *evaluation* of projects, not their design and formulation, it is assumed that

1. I. M. D. Little and J. A. Mirrlees, *Project Appraisal and Planning for Developing Countries* (New York: Basic Books, 1974); hereinafter referred to as OECD Manual.
2. P. Dasgupta, A. Sen, and S. Marglin, *Guidelines for Project Evaluation* (New York: United Nations, 1972); hereinafter referred to as UNIDO Manual.

the basic engineering and demand and cost analyses have been properly conducted for every project and every variant of every project which is to be evaluated."[3] The UNIDO Manual speaks of the necessity "to conserve the limited time of the project formulator by making a rational choice among the infinite number of alternative projects and project variants that could in principle be considered" without indicating on the basis of what methodology such rational choices should or can be made.[4]

A subsequent volume, produced by the World Bank in 1975, recognizes more explicitly the problems associated with project-by-project analysis under certain circumstances: "In many cases, however, a more direct link is necessary with the sector and economy as a whole: for example, the merit of a project characterized by economies of scale cannot be judged without making an estimate of the demand for its output, and this in turn requires placing the project in its sectoral and country context."[5] That text continues: "Consideration of alternatives is the single most important feature of proper project analysis throughout the project cycle, from the development plan for the particular sector through identification to appraisal. Many of the important choices are made at early stages when decisions are made concerning the alternatives that are to be rejected or retained for further, more detailed study."[6] The advice to project planners on how to deal effectively with this real problem, however, is once more put in very vague terms: "If economic analysis is to make a maximum contribution to the attempt to ensure that scarce resources are used to best advantage for the country, it should be used from the earliest phases of this process of successive sifting and narrowing down of options that are open to the country. The use of shadow prices reflecting basic policy objectives and resource constraints only in the final stage of appraisal, when most of the essential choices with respect to types of project and project design have already been made, tends to be mainly cosmetic. To be an effective aid in decision making, shadow prices should also be used in planning sector strategies and in identifying promising project possibilities and designing their

3. OECD Manual, pp. 10–11.
4. UNIDO Manual, p. 16.
5. Lyn Squire and Herman G. van der Tak, *Economic Analysis of Projects* (Baltimore: Johns Hopkins University Press, 1975), p. 17.
6. Ibid., p. 18.

major features."[7] These quotations state the problem admirably; once more, however, no guidelines on how to deal with these complications in practice are provided.

This volume seeks to redress the balance by outlining a systematic approach to the planning of industrial investment programs. The primary concern will be planning within one sector rather than across sectors. In this context, a project (or project variant) is defined as a scheme for investing resources with specific dimensions in terms of timing, scale, location, technology, and product mix. In other words, a steel plant of 1 million tons of raw steel capacity to be constructed in 1980 is one project, the same plant to be constructed in 1985 is another.

The main emphasis will be on the planning of projects in production activities that exhibit economies of scale in investment, that is, decreasing investment cost per unit of capacity as total capacity increases. In particular, we shall focus on production activities that offer a choice in terms of scale, timing, and location of capacity expansion; moreover, we shall explicitly recognize that different production technologies can be employed to produce a given good.

The Difficulty of Planning Investment Programs

The difficulty of planning investment programs stems from the fact that normally the project formulator faces a wide choice of alternative projects within a given sector. This necessitates adopting a procedure that can efficiently analyze and rank the alternative projects. It also requires the ability to handle a large amount of data.

The range of choices open to the project formulator is particularly wide if the productive activities under consideration exhibit economies of scale. In that case, the timing and scaling of productive capacity poses a difficult planning problem. If market requirements are growing over time, it may pay to postpone the construction of a plant until a large plant with lower average production costs is feasible and to make up the deficit in the meantime with imports. Alternatively, the construction of a plant with a certain initial overcapacity may be preferred, with the possibility of exporting the surplus. Moreover,

7. Ibid.

there is usually a trade-off between large production units with relatively high distribution costs but low production costs, and smaller, decentralized production units with relatively low distribution costs but higher average production costs. Also, problems are associated with the determination of the optimal product mix in a given plant or subsector, both from the point of view of raw material and intermediate product requirements and from that of the optimal use of multiproduct machinery. Generally, the most severe problem in project planning is to take account of the various forms of interdependence that frequently occur among productive activities. As indicated above, interdependence can occur over time and in space, as well as among products and productive units.

The difficulty of project planning ranges from manageable to enormous, depending on the production activities or set of activities. As an example, we can take the hypothetical case of a project planning problem that is defined as follows. Find the optimal investment program for a production activity:

- that can be located at any one or all of five sites;
- for which construction is to begin this year or next year;
- that can produce two possible product mixes; and
- that can rely on imports of the goods in question from overseas as an alternative to constructing domestic production capacity.

This seemingly simple planning problem turns out to be quite complex: in total, not less than 2^{20} project combinations, or more than 1 million, are possible! In practice, of course, project selection often offers an even wider set of choices, particularly if, in addition, interdependencies with other activities need to be taken into account, and if the project planning problem explicitly includes the selection of the appropriate scale. Since a large number of plant scales normally are possible, the number of project combinations can be expected to be greatly enlarged. In fact, if the range of possible plant scales is continuous, the number of project combinations becomes infinite.

The Apparent Ease of Project Planning in Some Circumstances

It is possible to conceive of circumstances under which project planning does not seem as difficult as was described in the previous section. As is clear from the definition of a project, the complexity of project planning depends on the range of choices the project formulator faces regarding each of the basic characteristics of a project. The choice may be limited by technical factors or by institutional constraints; moreover, firm rules of thumb may have been designed to guide the project selection process.

Technical restrictions

Sometimes the choice among different projects is restricted by technical factors. For example, no more than one production technology may exist; or not more than one site may need to be considered, for example, in the case of some dams. If, moreover, the activity in question does not exhibit economies of scale, the difficulty of the selection process is substantially reduced. Empirical studies have demonstrated, however, that a large number of production activities exhibit economies of scale in investment cost over some range of capacity levels.[8] In other cases, what may at first appear to be a technical restriction may simply reflect lack of adequate attention to defining alternatives. In practice, technical restrictions alone should rarely reduce the project selection problem to a trivial back-of-the-envelope exercise.

Institutional restrictions

Sometimes the problem of project selection is narrowed down by institutional restrictions, implicitly or explicitly expressed in the terms of reference of the project formulator; these may or may not represent legitimate noneconomic considerations. For example, the location of a project may be dictated by regional priorities that are given expression by the national policymakers. For prestige considerations, the latest technology may be prescribed. Most frequently, the policymakers may instruct the project formulator to come up with a project that can be implemented at once, even if postponement of the project to some future date may result in lower average cost of production.

---

8. See J. Haldi and D. Whitcomb, "Economies of Scale in Industrial Plants," *Journal of Political Economy*, 75 (August 1967), pp. 373–85; F. T. Moore, "Economies of Scale: Some Statistical Evidence," *Quarterly Journal of Economics*, 73 (May 1959), pp. 232–45; L. F. Pratten, *Economies of Scale in Manufacturing Industry* (London: Cambridge University Press, 1971); A. Silberston, "Economies of Scale in Theory and Practice," *Economic Journal*, 82 (March 1972, supplement), pp. 368–91.

It may be assumed, however, that the policymaker could change his mind if the cost difference between project or program variants were substantial. It may be argued that one of the tasks of the project planner is to inform the policymaker of the cost implications of institutionally imposed restrictions on project selection.

Rules of thumb

Special rules of thumb may have been designed to guide project planning in given sectors. Many such rules of thumb exist and they are of widely varying quality. For example, it is often asserted that industry based on imported raw materials should be located near the coast; in the same vein, industry based on local raw materials should be located near the raw material deposit. Also, the latest available technology is often selected because it is assumed, without further verification, to be the most efficient. The problem of timing of plant construction is sometimes solved simply by recommending construction as soon as the market for the plant's output is large enough to permit production at cost below the import price. Finally, rules of thumb abound with respect to the determination of the size of investment projects, usually taking the form of respecting "the minimum efficient scale." For example, commonly accepted minimum plant sizes are: 600–1,000 tons a day of ammonia production and 1,500–2,000 tons a day of cement clinker. One of the main theses of this volume will be that many rules of thumb used in project selection are invalid and, in fact, are unnecessary if a more systematic approach is taken to this phase in project planning.

A Systematic Approach to Project Planning under Economies of Scale

Although investment cost is characterized by diseconomies of scale in some industries, economies of scale are evident in most industries. Therefore, most of the attention in this book is given to the economies-of-scale case. The approach to project planning presented in this volume relies on a numerical technique that permits the systematic screening of large numbers of alternative project configurations and the selection of those which are superior to others relative to a given selection criterion. The technique employed is that of mixed-integer programming. The application of this technique requires a simplified representation of both the set of productive activities under consideration and the environment in which this set of activities is supposed to be carried out. Such a representation normally necessitates the use of a large number of variables and parameters, some of an area-specific nature, others of a technical engineering nature. It is also necessary to decide upon a selection criterion on the basis of which a choice can be made from among the many alternative projects that are normally possible. The selection criterion chosen here is minimization of cost, taking time into account.

Mixed-integer programming is only one of many ways to carry out formal investment analysis of industrial projects. For example, dynamic programming methods have been used by analysts to study essentially similar problems.[9] Both methods have their strengths and weaknesses, but improvements are continually being made. At the time our research was undertaken, it appeared that mixed-integer programming offered the best prospects for the efficient handling of industrial investment planning problems under economies of scale, where location, technology, and capacity-sizing are the major characteristics. Where the dominant concern is timing, or uncertainty, however, dynamic programming may be preferred.

The numerical techniques to be used, the data requirements, and the application possibilities will be described in detail in subsequent chapters. It may be useful now, however, to point out some basic features of the approach, as well as to emphasize that there remain certain shortcomings that need to be taken into account when evaluating the methodology.

The standard objective of the project selection problem under this approach is to meet specified market requirements with the minimum use of resources. The extent to which this basic formulation can be elaborated depends on the availability of data and on the dimensions of the project planning problem as perceived by the project formulator. The choice set may include imports versus domestic production,

9. See, for example, Alan S. Manne, ed., *Investments for Capacity Expansion: Size, Location and Time-Phasing* (Cambridge, Mass.: The M.I.T. Press, 1967); D. Erlenkotter, "The Sequencing of Interdependent Hydroelectric Projects" (Operations Research Study Center, University of California, Los Angeles, July 1972; processed); Y. Albouy and others, "An Integrated Planning Method for Power Systems" (Power Industry Computer Applications Meeting, New Orleans, June 1975; processed).

as well as various locations of production and demand, technologies, time periods, and product mixes. Most important, in the presence of economies of scale, the choice of the appropriate size of plants may be left open within a reasonable range. If full advantage is taken of the methodology, the project selection model will give the timing, scale, location, technology, and product mix of an investment program that can meet given market requirements at the lowest total resource cost (taking into account interdependencies among the individual productive activities in the set).

Given the aspects of project planning that can be addressed explicitly using the project selection model, it appears that the approach represents an advance over most commonly used methods of project selection. The methods proposed in this volume are not, however, without their imperfections, and further research is required to improve the present state of the art. One shortcoming relates to the selection criterion. Although there is not much wrong with a criterion that emphasizes the desirability of producing a given output with the minimum use of resources, it is not necessarily the only criterion on the basis of which projects should be selected. To the extent that other criteria are applied in project *evaluation*, it is necessary to ensure that, during the project selection phase, no project variants that deserve consideration during the evaluation phase will be eliminated. The next section will address itself explicitly to this question.

Another shortcoming of the proposed methodology is that market requirements are postulated. As the demand for most goods is affected by the price of the goods (that is, the demand faces nonzero price elasticities of demand), the price assumption underlying the estimate of market requirements is crucial. An adequate discussion of this issue is not possible until after the project selection methodology has been described; at this stage, therefore, we shall confine ourselves to alerting the reader that the treatment of final demand in the project selection model may pose problems.

A final major problem related to the project selection methodology to be described is that the data requirements for its full application are substantial. Although this requirement is in itself not a shortcoming, it may render the application of the full-fledged project selection model impossible in a number of cases. All that can be said in such cases is that the project selection model provides an indication of the types of data that are required for detailed project selection. It may be added here that improvements in data collection usually follow from the demonstration of the relevance of certain data to decisionmaking; such a demonstration can be made through improvements in analytical methods.

The Criterion for Project Selection

The selection of projects from among alternatives will be based on the criterion of minimization of cost. In principle, therefore, the result of a project selection model is the least-cost investment program. This program is not necessarily the one which is the most attractive on the basis of criteria that are more commonly used in the project evaluation phase, such as the internal rate of return or the discounted cash flow; it is even less representative if other project implications—such as employment, income distribution, or foreign exchange earnings—are taken into account in the evaluation phase. How, therefore, is project selection related to project evaluation? If all elements that play a role in the project evaluation phase could be incorporated into the project selection model criterion, the two phases in project planning would be merged into one, and the result of the model's application would be a single project or program.

It is doubtful whether this merger is desirable, even if it were possible. First, the employment of criteria that are more conventional in project evaluation not only would greatly complicate the structure of project selection models but also would increase the data requirements. Second, one of the main advantages of the project selection model is that it can be used to report upon a number of alternative investment projects or programs, which can be ranked in terms of total cost. During the project evaluation phase, these projects or programs can then be evaluated taking any other relevant criteria into account and, as a result, another ranking may be determined. One of the criteria that may influence the ranking of projects is the scope for revisions in the investment program over time. Given the uncertainty associated with the estimation and projection of variables and parameters, this aspect may be quite important in the selection of a specific program.

Two objections may be raised at this point. The first is that the project selection model, employed in this manner, may come up with a large number of alternative projects. The other is that the cutoff point may be wrongly selected so that projects that should be considered during the evaluation phase are rejected during the selection phase. The two objections are closely related and will therefore be dealt with together.

Assume that the project selection model is applied to a set of products that can be imported from abroad and for which the desirability of domestic production must be determined on the basis of a comparison between domestic production cost and import cost. The latter represent the cutoff point in the sense that any project combination that implies higher total cost than an all-import policy is rejected from the set of alternatives deserving consideration. It is quite possible that under these circumstances the project selection model results in a large number of alternative projects that have total cost associated with them that are below the cutoff point. In such cases, it is necessary to narrow the choice set further. Several possibilities that may be appropriate, depending on the particular situation, present themselves. One is to have only those projects reported upon which are within a specified range of the least-cost project or program. Incidentally, this may also be the procedure to adopt in the case of a productive activity that does not compete with imports, for instance, an irrigation project. Alternatively, certain "threshold" values may be introduced into the planning problem. For example, the cost of capital may be raised so that the project selection model comes up only with project combinations that cover this higher cost of capital. Similarly, a budget constraint may be introduced that forces the project selection model to investigate the feasibility of an investment program under more or less restrictive circumstances with regard to availability of capital. Also, threshold values may be introduced regarding foreign exchange earnings, employment, and so forth. It should be noted that the introduction of multiple thresholds may severely limit the number of feasible investment programs.

Normally, the cutoff point used in a project selection model that incorporates internationally tradable goods is the import cost; in the case of nontradables, the cutoff point may be a specified percentage above the cost of the least-cost program. The use of the import price as a measure of the opportunity cost of domestic production is now widely accepted by project analysts; in practice, however, the frequent occurrence of protective import duties suggests that this cutoff point may well be too restrictive in certain circumstances. The cost range selected in the case of nontradables is arbitrary, and it can easily be modified if desired. Nevertheless, the choice of the cutoff point has a direct impact on the number of feasible project combinations. Too restrictive a cutoff point will severely limit the number of projects, thus reducing the chance that an acceptable project combination can be identified by the policymaker when his choice is influenced by considerations other than cost alone. On the other hand, if the cutoff point is too liberal, one may be faced with a situation in which so many project combinations are feasible that a rational choice among them is almost impossible.

In summary, the project selection model based on minimization of cost enables the identification of alternative investment programs that meet given requirements at a cost below a specified cutoff point, but restrictions may have to be imposed on the selection procedure if a large number of project combinations appear feasible. To ensure that no projects are rejected that deserve consideration in the evaluation phase, multiple thresholds may be introduced, as long as they are assigned values that do not conflict with acceptable minimum standards applied in the evaluation phase. For example, if the project evaluation criterion includes a minimum rate of return on capital of 15 percent, a higher threshold value should not be assigned to the interest rate, because this might lead to the rejection of projects that are perfectly acceptable. In most cases, the careful selection of such thresholds will narrow the choice of project combinations to a manageable set. If this is not the case, a pragmatic alternative is to start off with the least-cost investment program and gradually to add project combinations with increasing cost until a program is identified that meets the minimum standards of the project analyst.

Previous Work on Project Planning under Economies of Scale

Ever since Adam Smith discerned the relation of productive efficiency to the size of the market, the occurrence of increasing returns to scale in several, mainly nonagricultural activities, has occupied economists. Earlier discussions of this phenomenon have focused primarily on the implications of increasing returns to scale on market structure and optimal pricing policies. Papers by Allyn Young and Frank Knight are among the first systematic contributions to this area, whereas P. N. Rosenstein-Rodan was the first to draw attention to the implications of economies of scale resulting from indivisibilities for resource allocation in economic planning.[10] The development of quantitative methods to incorporate economies of scale explicitly into project planning was begun by Hollis Chenery, first by a study of the effects of economies of scale on the optimal timing of capacity construction for natural gas transmission, in which it was demonstrated that total costs could be minimized by investment in overcapacity initially, followed by a study that focused on the need for simultaneous analysis of interdependent projects that are subject to economies of scale.[11]

Chenery's contributions in this area are in many respects the foundation on which much of the subsequent research on planning with economies of scale is based. Alan Manne extended the methodology developed for the natural gas transmission problem to include probabilistic demand growth and the choice between domestic production and imports.[12] Thomas Vietorisz and Manne considered the effects of economies of scale on the spatial location of projects and analyzed the optimal location of capacity in the South American fertilizer industry;[13] they applied a methodology developed by H. M. Markowitz and Manne based on the use of mathematical programming techniques in project planning under economies of scale.[14] Manne and others proceeded to study the optimal time-phasing, scaling, and location of several industrial activities in India.[15] At about the same time, David Kendrick developed a multiproduct, multiperiod model of the

10. See Allyn A. Young, "Increasing Returns and Economic Progress," *The Economic Journal*, 38 (1928), pp. 527–42; Frank H. Knight, "Some Fallacies in the Interpretation of Social Cost," *The Quarterly Journal of Economics*, 38 (1924), pp. 582–606; P. N. Rosenstein-Rodan, "Problems of Industrialization of Eastern and South Eastern Europe," *The Economic Journal*, 53 (1943), pp. 202–11.

11. Hollis B. Chenery, "Over-capacity and the Acceleration Principle," *Econometrica*, 20 (January 1952), pp. 1–28; and "The Interdependence of Investment Decisions," in *The Allocation of Economic Resources*, ed. M. Abramovitz (Stanford, Calif.: Stanford University Press, 1959).

12. Alan S. Manne, "Capacity Expansion and Probabilistic Growth," *Econometrica*, 24 (October 1961), pp. 632–49.

13. Thomas Vietorisz and Alan S. Manne, "Chemical Processes, Plant Location, and Economies of Scale," in *Studies in Process Analysis, Economy-wide Production Capabilities,* eds. Manne and H. M. Markowitz (New York: John Wiley, 1963).

14. H. M. Markowitz and Alan S. Manne, "On the Solution of Discrete Programming Problems," *Econometrica*, 25 (January 1957), pp. 84–110.

15. Manne, ed., *Investments for Capacity Expansion.*

Brazilian steel industry.[16] Larry Westphal subsequently developed a multisector model of the Korean economy in which special attention was paid to investments under economies of scale in the steel and petroleum sectors.[17] Following his earlier contribution to the 1967 volume edited by Manne, D. Erlenkotter produced a number of papers on the optimal sequencing of large-scale expansion projects.[18]

Following these earlier contributions, Ardy Stoutjesdijk, Charles Frank, Jr., and Alexander Meeraus developed a multicountry, multiproduct, dynamic model of the fertilizer industry in Kenya, Uganda, and Tanzania.[19] Among other things, they paid attention to the effect of economies of scale on investment decisions in common market areas. Westphal and Y. W. Rhee formulated a model of the multiproduct mechanical engineering industry in Korea that can be used to identify rapidly product lines for which domestic projects could possibly replace imported products.[20] In turn, H. G. Bergendorff built a model of the forest and forest industry sector, which he applied to both Turkey and a number of West African countries.[21] D. I. Gately constructed a model of part of the Indian electric power sector.[22] The first model to cover an industry (the fertilizer industry) on a worldwide basis, and to incorporate explicitly economies of scale, was recently developed by Meeraus, Stoutjesdijk, and Weigel.[23]

16. David Kendrick, *Programming Investment in the Process Industries: An Approach to Sectoral Planning* (Cambridge, Mass.: The M.I.T. Press, 1967).

17. Larry E. Westphal, *Planning Investments with Economies of Scale* (Amsterdam: North Holland Publishing Co., 1971).

18. See, for example, Erlenkotter, "The Sequencing of Interdependent Hydroelectric Projects."

19. Ardy Stoutjesdijk, Charles Frank, Jr., and Alexander Meeraus, "Planning in the Chemical Sector," in *Industrial Investment Analysis under Increasing Returns,* eds. Stoutjesdijk and Larry E. Westphal (forthcoming).

20. Larry E. Westphal and Y. W. Rhee, "A Model for Evaluating Investment Projects in the Mechanical Engineering Sector," in *Industrial Investment Analysis under Increasing Returns,* eds. Stoutjesdijk and Westphal.

21. H. G. Bergendorff, "A Model to Evaluate and Plan Projects in Forestry and Forest Industries" (Development Research Center, World Bank, March 1974; processed).

22. D. I. Gately, "Investment Planning for the Electric Power Industry: A Mixed-Integer Programming Approach, with Application to Southern India" (Ph.D. dissertation, Princeton University, 1971).

23. Alexander Meeraus, Ardy Stoutjesdijk, and Dale Weigel, "An Investment Planning Model for the World Fertilizer Industry" (World Bank, restricted circulation document; processed).

In summary, during the past two decades, the use of mathematical programming models for investment planning under economies of scale has developed from its single-period, single-product beginnings in a number of ways to include models with multiple (a) time periods, (b) products or sectors (taking into account interdependencies among them), and (c) markets. During the same period, large improvements have been made in the efficiency of both computers and solution procedures so that ever larger problems can be handled. There is every reason to expect that further improvements will be made, as a result of which the use of mathematical programming methods for project selection will increase. The present guidelines are produced to improve project selection by promoting a better understanding of the potential uses of these techniques and thus to assist both project analysts and development planners in the understanding and use of this category of development models.

A Reader's Guide to the Volume

The present volume describes a methodology for project planning in the presence of economies of scale. Chapter 2 gives a verbal description of the models to be used, proceeding from a simple transportation model through a process model to the full-scale project selection model. The intention of this chapter is only to give the reader a general flavor of the type of problems encountered in the area of project selection. Chapter 3 introduces some simple mathematics into the discussion, once more starting from the simplest case and gradually adding complexity to the problem. The presentation is self-contained, in the sense that no previous understanding of mathematical programming is needed to follow the argument.

The reader who already has some familiarity with process-analysis models or mathematical programming may wish to skip chapters 2 and 3 and move immediately to chapter 4, which contains a full mathematical statement of the project selection model. A frequently expressed objection to the use of mathematical programming models is that the data requirements are such that their application in developing countries is rarely possible. Chapter 5 addresses itself explicitly to this issue and, while listing the data needs specific to this type of model, indicates the tradeoff between the cost of collecting better and more data and the improvements in project selection procedures thus permitted.

Chapter 6 is in many respects the most important, for it deals with the uses of investment planning models. Apart from the obvious uses such as the design of an industrywide capacity expansion program (including plant location, the timing and scale of new capacity, and optimal shipment patterns between raw material source and plant, among plants, and between plant and consumer), this chapter describes how such models can be used for planning within an economic integration scheme among several countries and for the purpose of industry regulation.

The major limitations of the project selection model are discussed in chapter 7. To the extent possible, it indicates how several limitations can be removed by a change in the specification of the model. Chapter 8 focuses on methods of solution for project selection models with economies of scale. This chapter describes the approaches that can be followed to solve the model and includes a discussion of the calculations that can be carried out in the absence of a large-scale computer. Finally, chapter 9 highlights the issues raised in previous chapters and presents a summary of the volume.

2
A Description of the Model

A CONCISE VERBAL STATEMENT in this chapter describes the type of models with which this volume deals. First, a simple transport model is presented; then, a process model is described; and, finally, a complete project selection model is sketched. The mathematical development of similar models is presented in the next chapter, so the reader who has a certain familiarity with the scope and structure of project selection models may want to proceed immediately to chapter 3.

A Transport Model

The core of the transport model is the notion that most industrial products are produced at a relatively small number of factories and are purchased, for the most part, in a limited number of marketing centers. No factory can produce more than its capacity to produce; nor can it ship more output than it produces, assuming no inventories.[1] Each factory can potentially ship its output to any combina-

---

1. Generally, our models will not include inventories. Their absence can be justified on two grounds. First, the project selection model as presented in this volume does not normally incorporate uncertainty. Second, it will usually be more efficient to use temporary surplus capacity to export or produce for relatively distant domestic marketing centers rather than for the accumulation of inventories. It is only in the case of goods that cannot be exported—or in the case of a model that is not spatially disaggregated—that inventories need to be explicitly incorporated into the planning model.

tion of marketing centers. Similarly, each marketing center can receive products from any combination of factories and must receive at least as much in total as it is prepared to purchase.

In fact, not all factories ship to all marketing centers; rather, in both market economies and centrally planned economies, plants tend to ship only to nearby marketing centers. This may result from profit motives in the market economy, or from efficiency motives on the part of planners in the centrally planned economy. This phenomenon can be reproduced in a model that seeks to find the set of shipments from plants to markets that will minimize the total transportation costs required to ship the product from plant to market. This is diagrammed in figure 1, which shows both all potential shipments from plants to markets and the least-cost shipments.

Thus, the transport model simply specifies that:

- Each plant ships no more than it produces;
- No plant produces more of a product than its capacity to produce that product; and
- Each marketing center receives no more of each product than it wishes to purchase.

The model can be expanded to cover several time periods (for example, years) by imposing constraints on plant capacity and market requirements for each time period. One then solves the model by seeking to find the shipments from plants to markets that minimize the present value of transport costs.

Bringing Production Cost into the Model

The model can easily be expanded to take the production cost at each plant into account. This is desirable if production cost differ from plant to plant.

To minimize total cost associated with market requirements in each market, it is now necessary to minimize the sum of average production cost in each plant plus the total transport cost required to ship the product from plant to market. Plants that enjoy a transport cost advantage in a given market, as compared with other plants, may lose this advantage, wholly or partly, as a result of differences in average production costs.

To increase the realism of the model, it can be generalized to in-

Figure 1. Shipments from Plants to Markets

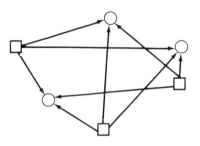

All potential shipments

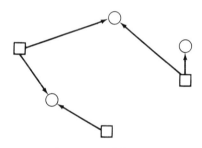

Least-cost shipments

☐ Plants   ◯ Markets

corporate more than one product, because few industries produce a single product. The determination of the least-cost supply pattern will now have to be performed for each product in the model.

A Process Model

If, in trying to implement the transport model, one visited a factory in order to determine its capacity for each of a number of different products, one would surely encounter engineers who insisted that it is not products that have capacities but rather machines or productive units, and that each product requires a certain amount of processing time on a machine or in a productive unit. Thus, the model is constructed so that a number of different products can be produced at each plant: nevertheless, the model does not permit the mix and quantity of products produced to exceed the available capacity of each machine.

This augmented model seems perfectly adequate until it is discovered that raw materials in many industries are used to produce intermediate products. The latter are then combined to fabricate final products, which are subsequently shipped to markets. For example, natural gas is used to produce ammonia, and elemental sulfur is used to produce sulfuric acid. These intermediate products are then used in a fertilizer plant to produce ammonium sulfate. Such circumstances require: (a) that the quantity of raw materials required to produce intermediate products be specified, as well as the quantity of raw materials and intermediates required to produce final products; and (b) that relations be introduced into the model requiring that the supply of each raw material and intermediate good is sufficient for its usage in final products.

Next, the relationships among raw materials, intermediate products, and final products should be expressed in the form of technical or input-output coefficients. For example, the production of 1 metric ton of sulfuric acid (an intermediate product) requires 0.335 metric tons of elemental sulfur (a raw material), whereas the production of 1 metric ton of single superphosphate (a final product, at least in the fertilizer industry) requires 0.4 metric tons of sulfuric acid (an intermediate good) and 0.6 metric tons of phosphate rock (a raw material).

The capacity constraints of certain machines (productive units) may limit the amount of intermediate products that can be produced and thus, in turn, limit the production of final products.

In industries of this type, it is frequently observed that, although some plants may be fully integrated in the sense that they produce all of the intermediates and all of the final products, many are not. The latter ship intermediate products to one another. This feature is also incorporated into the model via the balance constraint, except that this constraint requires that the production of an intermediate good cannot be less than its usage. This constraint is now generalized to require that the production of each intermediate product plus the shipments received from other plants cannot be less than the amount shipped to other plants plus the amount used in producing final goods in the plant itself.

Raw materials and intermediate goods inputs are usually directly proportional to the level of production of final goods. The same applies to most of the other recurrent cost categories such as electric power, fuel oil, cooling water, and the like.[2] The recurrent cost categories need to be specified separately only if there is reason to assume that their availability in the required amounts may be restricted. If this is not the case, recurrent cost categories may be lumped together, for any specific process, and expressed per unit of output. This can be done only if the cost per unit for such categories can be assumed to be constant, regardless of the quantity used.

In summary, the process model consists of a set of plants and a set of markets. Each plant has associated with it a set of productive units, each with its own capacity. There are three types of products in the model: raw materials, intermediate products, and final products. The raw materials are purchased for use in manufacturing the intermediate and final products, and the intermediate products are used to produce final products; intermediate products may be shipped among plants, whereas final products are shipped to the marketing centers. The recurrent costs of production at each plant are the cost of the raw materials, the cost of any intermediate products that are purchased from other plants, and the cost of labor and other recurrent cost categories such as power, water, insurance, and so forth. Transport costs include those incurred in shipments of (a) raw materials to plants, (b) intermediate products between plants, and (c) final products from plants to markets. As before, the objective or criterion of the model is to determine the levels of production in each plant and the levels of shipments that will minimize the production and transport costs of meeting given market requirements.

As yet, the model has included no allowance for imports and exports, in spite of the fact that they frequently play a substantial role. Imports of raw materials and intermediate products add to the domestic availability of these categories for further processing, and imports of final products to markets are an alternative source of meeting market requirements. Exports of intermediate and final products lower

---

2. If recurrent cost categories are proportional not to output (for example, plant insurance, some categories of labor, and so forth) but rather to capacity of the plant, they have to be treated as overhead costs. In that event, their treatment in the model is different and resembles the treatment of investment cost, which will be described later.

the domestic availability of such products. Import cost is added to production and transport cost, and export revenue is subtracted from them. Imports are usually assumed to be available in unlimited quantities at a given price, whereas export possibilities are restricted to a given level and face an attainable price that is less than the import price.

A Project Selection Model

So far, all capital costs have been neglected, and capacity has been assumed to be fixed. Although the incorporation of investments to augment capacity makes the model more complicated, it is the indispensable condition for the selection of investment projects. To do this, investment activities that create new capacity or add to existing capacity in the various productive units at each plant in each time period may be introduced. For example, a typical investment activity might be a project for the construction of an additional basic oxygen furnace (BOF) converter in the steel shop of the USIMINAS plant in Brazil in 1980. Thus, each investment activity is specified by the productive unit, the plant, and the time period. The amount of capacity added via the activity may be either fixed, when equipment sizes are standardized (for example, kilns for clinker production), or continuous, when productive units of any size may be ordered.

Now, at last, economies of scale will be introduced explicitly into the model. Investment costs per unit of capacity typically decrease with the size of the productive unit. Thus, the concentration of capacity at one large plant, rather than at a number of small plants, makes it possible to incur a smaller total capital cost per unit of output. This incentive to centralize is offset, however, by increasing transport costs, because final products must be shipped over greater distances to markets. Similarly, there is an incentive to add large productive units at infrequent time intervals rather than small units at frequent time intervals. The counterpressure here comes from the fact that large units at infrequent time intervals imply more unused capacity with a temporarily higher capital cost. These, then, are the two primary economic implications of economies of scale. They produce incentives to have large intervals between productive units in both space and time, and these incentives are traded off against transport cost and interest cost, respectively.

The possibility of capacity expansion necessitates taking into account capital costs associated with capacity construction. As the planning period in which the project planner is interested is often shorter than the lifetime of the capacity, the total investment cost needs to be converted into a periodic charge so as to ensure that no capital costs that properly belong to later years are imputed. The simplest way to visualize this is to assume that the plant and equipment representing the capacity expansion are available at a rental charge, which includes not only the original cost of the equipment but also the interest charges on capital. The formula for computing this rental charge is the capital recovery factor.[3]

The treatment of exports in a project selection model incorporating economies of scale deserves special mention. If the scope for exports at a given price were unlimited, infinitely large plant sizes might be recommended. For this reason, it is necessary to introduce realistic bounds on exports, which may increase over time if it seems appropriate to assume that export markets will be captured during the planning period. Alternatively, a declining marginal price for exports can be assumed.

The complete project selection model may now be described as a model that seeks to find the levels of production, shipment activities, imports and exports, and investment activities that will minimize the costs of meeting the market requirements over a period of time without violating the constraints imposed by domestic demand requirements, by export demands, and by the productive capacities of the units in the plants.

---

3. We are indebted to one of the reviewers of the manuscript for pointing out that the central approach used in this book may be misleading in cases in which the deterioration in capital equipment is related to use more than to the simple passage of time, and that the use of the equipment may be much higher in its early years than in its later years. Attention is called to these issues by using terminal capital stocks and focusing explicitly on expected usage rates both before and after the terminal period.

3

Mathematical Development
of the Model

FROM A SIMPLE TRANSPORT MODEL, this chapter progresses to a multiproduct, dynamic investment planning model by way of a set of other models of intermediate complexity. The next chapter, on the complete model, is self-contained, with a full listing of variables and a statement of constraints; the reader who is already familiar with mathematical models of this type may turn directly to chapter 4.

A Transport Model

An investment planning model can gradually be developed by starting with the plants and markets that produce and consume a specific commodity. Any plant can serve any market, but one ordinarily observes that plants tend to serve nearby markets. This may result either from competitive forces or from the desire for efficiency in a centrally planned economy. One can model this phenomenon by seeking to find which plants would serve which markets if total transport cost were to be minimized, without permitting any plant to ship more than its capacity to produce or any market to receive less than it requires.

Let:

i = an individual plant in the set of plants I;

j = an individual market in the set of markets J;

x_{ij} = the amount of the good shipped from plant i to market j;

k_i = the capacity of plant i.

Then, the logical necessity that no plant can ship more than its capacity can be written as:

$$(3.1) \qquad \sum_{j \epsilon J} x_{ij} \leq k_i, \qquad\qquad i \epsilon I$$

that is, the sum of shipments from each plant i to all markets must be less than or equal to the capacity of plant i. In (3.1):

- the symbol ϵ indicates membership in a set;
- the statement $\sum_{j \epsilon J}$ indicates that one should add over the indexes contained in the set J (in this case markets);
- the symbol $<$ indicates less than or equal to;
- the symbols $i \epsilon I$ on the right indicate that there must be a constraint of type (3.1) for each plant i.

Consider an example with three marketing centers and two plants. Then, the sets J and I can be written as $J = \{1, 2, 3\}$ and $I = \{1, 2\}$, so that (3.1) is written as:

$$x_{11} + x_{12} + x_{13} \leq k_1,$$
$$x_{21} + x_{22} + x_{23} \leq k_2.$$

This requires that the total of shipments from plant 1 to markets 1, 2, and 3 be less than or equal to the capacity of plant 1, and that shipments from plant 2 to markets 1, 2, and 3 be less than or equal to the capacity of plant 2.

The other constraint of the transport model is that each market should receive at least as much as it wants to purchase at current price and income levels. Let:

d_j = the requirement of market j.

Then, the market requirement constraint can be written as:

$$(3.2) \qquad \sum_{i \epsilon I} x_{ij} \geq d_j, \qquad\qquad j \epsilon J$$

that is, the summation of shipments from all plants i to each market

j must be equal to or greater than the product requirement of market j.[1] For the example above with three markets and two plants, these constraints are written as:

$$x_{11} + x_{21} \geq d_1,$$
$$x_{12} + x_{22} \geq d_2,$$
$$x_{13} + x_{23} \geq d_3.$$

Finally, shipments x_{ij} cannot assume negative values. This is formally stated in the mathematical structure of the model by nonnegativity constraints:

(3.3) $x_{ij} \geq 0.$ $i \epsilon I$
                                                                        $j \epsilon J$

The objective or criterion of this problem is to minimize the transport cost while satisfying the sets of constraints (3.1), (3.2), and (3.3). Let:

μ_{ij} = the constant unit transport cost for shipping the product from plant i to market j.

Then, the cost of transportation of shipment x_{ij}, from plant i to market j is equal to:

$$\mu_{ij} x_{ij},$$

and the criterion of minimizing total cost may be stated as minimizing ξ, where:

(3.4) $\xi = \sum_{i \epsilon I} \sum_{j \epsilon J} \mu_{ij} x_{ij}.$

This term represents the sum of the transport costs associated with all shipments from plants i to markets j. For the three-market,

---

1. Normally, this constraint can be thought of as an equality, since it would obviously not be consistent with the cost-minimizing objective to supply more to any market than its requirements. Sometimes, however, oversupply is inevitable for technical reasons, for example, in the case of goods that are produced and shipped in fixed proportions. For example, several chemical fertilizers contain both nitrogen and phosphorus nutrients. If market requirements are stated in terms of nutrients, it is obviously not always possible to meet requirements for both nutrients exactly, and oversupply of one of them often occurs. The general formulation of (3.2) anticipates such situations.

two-plant example, (3.4) would be written as:

$$\min \xi = (\mu_{11}x_{11} + \mu_{12}x_{12} + \mu_{13}x_{13}) + (\mu_{21}x_{21} + \mu_{22}x_{22} + \mu_{23}x_{23}).$$

In summary, the simple transport model is to select x_{ij} to minimize total transport costs:

$$(3.5) \qquad\qquad \min \xi = \sum_{i \epsilon I} \sum_{j \epsilon J} \mu_{ij} \, x_{ij} ,$$

subject to the capacity constraints (3.1), the market requirements constraints (3.2), and the nonnegativity constraints (3.3).

Bringing Production Cost into the Model

The transport model can be extended to take production cost into account. Initially, we shall focus on the simplest case; average production cost per unit of product is assumed to be constant. Let:

θ_i = the average production cost for the product of plant i.

Then, the total production cost per plant i are:

$$\theta_i \sum_{j \epsilon J} x_{ij} .$$

The necessary modification of the criterion of the model is the addition of production cost summed over all plants, as follows:

$$(3.6) \qquad \min \xi = \sum_{i \epsilon I} \sum_{j \epsilon J} \mu_{ij} \, x_{ij} + \sum_{i \epsilon I} \left(\theta_i \sum_{j \epsilon J} x_{ij} \right),$$

$$= \sum_{i \epsilon I} \sum_{j \epsilon J} x_{ij} \, (\mu_{ij} + \theta_i),$$

where the first term represents the by now familiar total shipment costs and the second term represents the total production costs. The economics of this problem are in the tradeoff between production cost and transportation cost. If one of the plants has much lower production costs than the others (perhaps because of a favorable location near a rich raw material deposit), then it may be able to absorb the transport cost and still deliver products to relatively distant markets at a lower total cost than nearby plants. Constraints (3.1), (3.2), and (3.3) remain unchanged.

Because few industries produce a single product, the model is next generalized to a multiproduct form.

A Multiproduct Model

The simplest form of the multiproduct model is to add a subscript c to represent the commodities produced in the industry. Let:

C = the set of commodities produced in the industry; and

x_{cij} = the amount of commodity c shipped from plant i to market j.

Then, the model is to select x_{cij} so as to minimize:

$$(3.7) \qquad \min \xi = \sum_{c \in C} \left(\sum_{i \in I} \sum_{j \in J} \mu_{cij} \, x_{cij} + \sum_{i \in I} \theta_{ci} \sum_{j \in J} x_{cij} \right),$$

which is the sum of all shipment costs from all plants i to all markets j, for all commodities c, plus the production cost for all commodities c at plants i, subject to:

CAPACITY CONSTRAINTS

$$(3.8) \qquad\qquad \sum_{j \in J} x_{cij} \leq k_{ci} \qquad\qquad \begin{aligned} & c \in C \\ & i \in I \end{aligned}$$

MARKET REQUIREMENTS

$$(3.9) \qquad\qquad \sum_{i \in I} x_{cij} \geq d_{cj} \qquad\qquad \begin{aligned} & c \in C \\ & j \in J \end{aligned}$$

NONNEGATIVITY CONSTRAINTS

$$(3.10) \qquad\qquad x_{cij} \geq 0 \qquad\qquad \begin{aligned} & c \in C \\ & i \in I \\ & j \in J \end{aligned}$$

The constraints are analogous to the previous constraints (3.1), (3.2), and (3.3), but now each market's requirements and each plant's capacity are expressed for each commodity, thus allowing for the possibility that a plant produces more than one commodity.

This model is unsatisfactory, however, because capacity is normally associated with productive units or machines rather than with products. This is because many products require processing by a variety of different machines and because many machines are capable of producing a spectrum of different products. Therefore, the capacity of the plant in terms of products is not a well-defined concept. In contrast, the capacity of a machine in terms of the number of hours of its availability, or the volume of throughput, is usually well defined.

To specify the model in this form, let:

z_{ci} = the production of commodity c at plant i;

M = the set of machines (productive units), where m is an individual machine in the set;

b_{mci} = the number of units (namely, hours) of capacity used on machine or productive unit m per unit of output of commodity c at plant i.

The model may now be stated as: select x_{cij} and z_{ci} so as to minimize the sum of shipment and production costs. That is,

$$(3.11) \qquad \min \xi = \sum_{c \epsilon C} \left(\sum_{i \epsilon I} \sum_{j \epsilon J} \mu_{cij} x_{cij} + \sum_{i \epsilon I} \theta_{ci} z_{ci} \right),$$

$$= \sum_{c \epsilon C} \sum_{i \epsilon I} \left(\sum_{j \epsilon J} \mu_{cij} x_{cij} + \theta_{ci} z_{ci} \right),$$

subject to a set of constraints. The first of these constraints, (3.12), is new; the others correspond to (3.1) to (3.3), and (3.8) to (3.10). The first two constraints are:

MATERIAL BALANCE CONSTRAINTS

$$(3.12) \qquad\qquad z_{ci} \geq \sum_{j \epsilon J} x_{cij}, \qquad\qquad \begin{array}{l} c \epsilon C \\ i \epsilon I \end{array}$$

that is, production of commodity c at plant i must be greater than or equal to shipments of commodity c from plant i to all markets j. This constraint exists for each plant i and for all commodities c.

CAPACITY CONSTRAINTS

$$(3.13) \qquad\qquad \sum_{c \epsilon C} b_{mci} z_{ci} \leq k_{mi} \qquad\qquad \begin{array}{l} m \epsilon M \\ i \epsilon I \end{array}$$

This replaces the previous constraint (3.8). Capacity is now defined as k_{mi} rather than as k_{ci} in the previous model. This denotes the change of capacity from a commodity characteristic to a machine characteristic. Production levels for all commodities at plant i should be such that capacity usage does not exceed capacity availability in any productive unit m in plant i. It should be noted that the coefficient b_{mci} in (3.13) will be positive when a commodity requires a particular machine for its production and zero when the machine is not required.

Finally, two constraints correspond to the previous constraints (3.9) and (3.10). The only difference is that there is an additional nonnegativity constraint for z_{ci}. These two constraints are:

MARKET REQUIREMENTS

$$(3.14) \qquad \sum_{i \in I} x_{cij} \geq d_{cj} \qquad\qquad c \in C \\ j \in J$$

NONNEGATIVITY CONSTRAINTS

$$(3.15) \qquad x_{ij}, z_{ci} \geq 0 \qquad\qquad i \in I \\ i \in J \\ c \in C$$

A Process Model

In many industries, the above model is inadequate because intermediate commodities are produced and used in the plants. These intermediate commodities are not shipped to markets but are the products that use productive capacity. Also, in some industries, there is a substantial trade among plants in these intermediate products, and for those industries it is important to represent such trade explicitly in the model.

At this point, it is helpful to generalize the notion of production from the output of commodity z_{ci} to the activity level of a process z_{pi}, where

z_{pi} = the activity level of process p at plant i.

The notion of a process is introduced for two reasons. First, it permits the description of production methods that create more than one product or by-product. An example is the electrolysis of sodium chloride, which produces both sodium hydroxide and chlorine gas. Second, it makes it possible to introduce alternative processes for producing the same good into the model: for example, the production of pig iron with either regular ore, sinter, or pellets, or the production of electric power with either coal, natural gas, or petroleum. By explicitly representing alternative processes in the model, the model can be used to analyze the shift in resource utilization in response to changes in relative prices.

The collection of all possible processes is defined as:

P = the set of processes in use.

For example, the set of processes in a textile mill might be spinning, weaving, and dyeing.

To specify processes, let:

a_{cpi} = the input $(-)$ or output $(+)$ of commodity c by process p at plant i per unit level of activity of process p.

For example, consider the process of producing the chemical fertilizer of single superphosphate. Such a process has phosphate rock, sulfuric acid, and labor as its main inputs, and electric power and unspecified supplies as its miscellaneous inputs. In such a case, one could have:

a_{cpi} = 1.0 ton c = single superphosphate
a_{cpi} = -0.6 ton c = phosphate rock
a_{cpi} = -0.36 ton c = sulfuric acid
a_{cpi} = -0.4 manhours c = labor
a_{cpi} = $-\$0.50$ c = miscellaneous material inputs

That is, the process combines 0.6 tons of phosphate rock, 0.36 tons of sulfuric acid, 0.4 manhours, and $0.50 worth of miscellaneous material inputs to produce 1 ton of single superphosphate.

In order to specify the process model, it is convenient to divide the commodities used or produced in the plant into five groups: final commodities that are shipped from plants to markets; intermediate commodities that are either produced within the plant or shipped among other plants; raw materials that are purchased by the plant from outside sources; raw materials or intermediates for which no separate specification is deemed necessary, referred to below as "miscellaneous material inputs"; and inputs of different types of labor. For the time being, the inputs of raw materials, other material inputs, and all labor types are considered directly variable with output, and they are lumped together into one category. Accordingly, the set of inputs and outputs C is divided into the subsets:

CF = final commodities,
CI = intermediate commodities,
CR = raw materials, miscellaneous material inputs, and labor inputs.

In the example above, the sets would be specified as follows:

> CF = single superphosphate,
> CI = sulfuric acid,
> CR = phosphate rock, electricity, miscellaneous supplies, and labor.

Since cost is no longer defined as attached to a final commodity, but rather to the various input categories, it is necessary to define:

> p_{ci} = the price of input c delivered to (or purchased at) plant i,
> u_{ci} = the amount of purchases of input c delivered to (or purchased at) plant i.

Thus:

(3.16) $\sum_{c \epsilon CR} p_{ci} u_{ci}$ = the cost of inputs to plant i.

With this notation, the process model may be specified as: select z_{pi}, x_{cij}, and u_{ci} so as to minimize the sum of total shipment costs and the total costs of raw materials, labor, and miscellaneous material inputs. That is,

(3.17) $\min \xi = \sum_{c \epsilon CF} \sum_{i \epsilon I} \sum_{j \epsilon J} \mu_{cij} x_{cij} + \sum_{c \epsilon CR} p_{ci} u_{ci}$,

subject to:

MATERIAL BALANCE CONSTRAINTS ON FINAL COMMODITIES

(3.18) $\sum_{p \epsilon P} a_{cpi} z_{pi} \geq \sum_{j \epsilon J} x_{cij}$. $\begin{matrix} c \epsilon CF \\ i \epsilon I \end{matrix}$

The production of commodity c by all processes p at plant i must at least equal the shipments of commodity c from plant i to all markets j. The typical process p that provides final commodities can be assigned a coefficient $a_{cpi} = 1.0$ in the final commodities constraint (3.18), because the unit of capacity can be arbitrarily defined in terms of one of the inputs or outputs.

MATERIAL BALANCE CONSTRAINTS ON INTERMEDIATE COMMODITIES

(3.19) $\sum_{p \epsilon P} a_{cpi} z_{pi} \geq 0$. $\begin{matrix} c \epsilon CI \\ i \epsilon I \end{matrix}$

The production of final products and some intermediate products processes p at plant i requires the use of intermediate products. At least one process p in constraint (3.19) will therefore have a negative coefficient a_{cpi}, while there has to be at least one process for producing an intermediate good that has a positive coefficient in the intermediate product constraint for the latter to hold. This assumes, for the time being, that there are no interplant shipments of intermediates.

MATERIAL BALANCE CONSTRAINTS ON RAW MATERIALS AND LABOR

$$(3.20) \qquad \sum_{p \epsilon P} a_{cpi} z_{pi} + u_{ci} \geq 0 . \qquad \begin{matrix} c \epsilon CR \\ i \epsilon I \end{matrix}$$

The production of intermediate and final products requires raw materials and labor. The coefficient a_{cpi} in constraint (3.20) will therefore normally be negative. Purchases of raw material and labor u_{ci}, in turn, will have to be positive for the constraint to hold.

CAPACITY CONSTRAINTS

$$(3.21) \qquad \sum_{p \epsilon P} b_{mpi} z_{pi} \leq k_{mi} , \qquad \begin{matrix} m \epsilon M \\ i \epsilon I \end{matrix}$$

where b_{mpi} is the number of units of capacity used on machine or productive unit m per unit of output of process p at plant i.

MARKET REQUIREMENTS

$$(3.22) \qquad \sum_{i \epsilon I} x_{cij} \geq d_{cj} ; \qquad \begin{matrix} c \epsilon CF \\ j \epsilon J \end{matrix}$$

NONNEGATIVITY CONSTRAINTS

$$(3.23) \qquad x_{cij}, z_{pi}, u_{ci} \geq 0. \qquad \begin{matrix} i \epsilon I \\ j \epsilon J \\ c \epsilon C \\ p \epsilon P \end{matrix}$$

Constraints (3.21) and (3.22) are essentially the same as before. The difference between final, intermediate, and raw material commodities is clearly shown in the material balance constraints (3.18), (3.19), and (3.20). Final goods are shipped to markets, intermediate goods production and use must be balanced within the plant, and raw materials must be purchased outside of the plant in sufficient quantities to equal at least their use in producing intermediate and final goods. Miscellaneous material inputs are by definition assumed to be available in sufficient quantities. Consequently, they appear in the criterion function only as a component of the set CR.

At this point, it may be helpful to restate, in alphabetical order, the sets and indexes, variables, and parameters used so far.

Symbol	*Definition*

SETS AND INDEXES

C	Set of commodities used or produced in the industry
CF	Final products
CI	Intermediate products
CR	Raw materials, miscellaneous material inputs, and labor inputs
I	Set of plants
J	Set of markets
M	Set of productive units
P	Set of production processes

VARIABLES

u	Purchases
x	Shipments
z	Production or process levels

PARAMETERS

a	Process inputs $(-)$ or outputs $(+)$
b	Capacity utilization
k	Capacity
p	Prices
d	Market requirements
θ	Unit production costs
μ	Unit transportation costs

Interplant Shipments, Exports, and Imports

Interplant shipments of intermediate materials are a common practice in a variety of industries. These shipments enter the balance equation for intermediate commodities, and they add a transport cost element to the criterion function. The shipments are defined with the notation:

$x_{cii'}$ = shipments of commodity c from plant i to plant i';
$\mu_{cii'}$ = unit costs for shipping commodity c from plant i to plant i'.

Exports and imports also play a substantial role in most industries.

The definition of exports and imports depends on the construction of the model, but they may generally be defined as shipment to or from sources outside of the plants, markets, and raw material sources explicitly defined in the model. Thus, for a model of a single company with several plants, export and import shipments would be to or from other companies. For a national model, the conventional definition of imports and exports would hold. For a multinational (or common market) model, imports and exports would constitute shipments to or from the set of countries not explicitly included in the model.

The model includes imports of raw materials and intermediate commodities to plants and of final products to markets. It also includes exports of intermediate and final commodities from plants. The notation used for these flows is as follows:

Symbol	Definition
v_{ci}	Imports of commodity c to plant i (raw materials and intermediates)
v_{cj}	Imports of commodity c to market j (final commodities)
e_{cil}	Exports of commodity c from plant i to export area l
L	Set of export markets
μ_{ci}	Unit transport cost for shipping imported commodity c from the appropriate port of entry to plant i
μ_{cj}	Unit transport cost for shipping imported commodity c from the appropriate port of entry to market j
μ_{cil}	Unit transport cost for shipping commodity c from plant i to the appropriate port of exit when the commodity is bound for export market l
p^v_{ci}	Import price of commodity c at the appropriate entry port when bound for plant i
p^v_{cj}	Import price of commodity c at the appropriate entry port when bound for market j
p^e_{cil}	Export price of commodity c at the appropriate exit port when bound from plant i to export market area l

Exports are labeled by destination l in order to permit the model to include discriminatory pricing.

For some industries, domestic sales of by-products are a significant source of revenues that may affect investment decisions. The notation used in the model to denote domestic sales and prices is:

w_{ci} = domestic sales of commodity c as a by-product;

p^d_{ci} = domestic price of commodity c at plant i.

In order to simplify the criterion function, it is necessary to divide the function into the following components:

ϕ_ψ = raw materials, miscellaneous material inputs, and labor costs;

ϕ_λ = transportation cost;

ϕ_π = import cost;

ϕ_ϵ = export revenue;

ϕ_x = revenue from domestic sale of by-products.

Then, the criterion function can be defined as the algebraic (plus and minus) sum of these terms, the first three being positive (costs) and the last two negative (revenues).

The model can now be restated as select z_{pi} (process levels), x_{cij} (shipments of final goods), $x_{cii'}$ (shipments of intermediate goods), e_{cil} (exports), v_{ci} (imports of raw materials and intermediates), v_{cj} (imports of final goods), w_{ci} (by-product sales), and u_{ci} (purchases of domestic inputs), so as to minimize:

$$(3.24) \qquad \min \xi = \phi_\psi + \phi_\lambda + \phi_\pi - \phi_\epsilon - \phi_x ,$$

where:

$$(3.25) \quad \phi_\psi = \sum_{c\epsilon CR} \sum_{i\epsilon I} p^d_{ci}\, u_{ci} ,$$

$$\begin{bmatrix} Input \\ costs \end{bmatrix} = \begin{bmatrix} Total\ costs\ of\ raw\ materials,\ labor,\ and \\ miscellaneous\ material\ inputs \end{bmatrix}$$

$$(3.26) \quad \phi_\lambda = \sum_{c\epsilon CF} \left(\sum_{i\epsilon I} \sum_{j\epsilon J} \mu_{cij}\, x_{cij} + \sum_{j\epsilon J} \mu_{cj}\, v_{cj} + \sum_{i\epsilon I} \sum_{l\epsilon L} \mu_{cil}\, e_{cil} \right)$$

$$+ \sum_{c\epsilon CI} \left(\sum_{i\epsilon I} \sum_{\substack{i'\epsilon I \\ i\neq i'}} \mu_{cii'}\, x_{cii'} + \sum_{i\epsilon I} \mu_{ci}\, v_{ci} + \sum_{i\epsilon I} \sum_{l\epsilon L} \mu_{cil}\, e_{cil} \right)$$

$$+ \sum_{c\epsilon CR} \left(\sum_{i\epsilon I} \mu_{ci}\, v_{ci} \right),$$

$$\begin{bmatrix} Transport \\ costs \end{bmatrix} = \begin{bmatrix} Total\ costs\ of\ transport\ of\ final \\ goods,\ intermediates,\ and\ raw \\ materials,\ including\ domestic \\ transport\ cost\ of\ imports\ and \\ exports;\ domestically\ purchased \\ raw\ materials\ are\ assumed\ to \\ be\ priced\ inclusive\ of\ domestic \\ transport\ cost \end{bmatrix}$$

$$(3.27) \quad \phi_\pi = \sum_{c\epsilon CF} \sum_{j\epsilon J} p^v_{cj} v_{cj} + \sum_{c\epsilon(CI \ \cup \ CR)} \sum_{i\epsilon I} p^v_{ci} v_{ci} ,$$

$$\begin{bmatrix} Import \\ cost \end{bmatrix} = \begin{bmatrix} Total \ cost \ of \ imports \ of \ final \ and \ intermediate \\ goods \ as \ well \ as \ raw \ materials, \ where \ the \\ notation \ CI \ \cup \ CR \ means \ the \ union \ of \ the \\ sets \ CI \ and \ CR, \ that \ is, \ the \ summation \ is \\ over \ all \ commodities \ that \ are \ either \ intermediate \\ products \ or \ raw \ materials \end{bmatrix}$$

$$(3.28) \quad \phi_\epsilon = \sum_{c\epsilon(CF \ \cup \ CI)} \sum_{i\epsilon I} \sum_{l\epsilon L} p^e_{cil} e_{cil} ,$$

$$\begin{bmatrix} Export \\ revenue \end{bmatrix} = \begin{bmatrix} Total \ revenue \ resulting \ from \ exports \ of \\ final \ and \ intermediate \ goods \end{bmatrix}$$

$$(3.29) \quad \phi_\chi = \sum_{c\epsilon CI} \sum_{i\epsilon I} p^d_{ci} w_{ci} ,$$

$$\begin{bmatrix} By\text{-}product \\ revenue \end{bmatrix} = \begin{bmatrix} Total \ revenue \ resulting \ from \ the \ sale \\ of \ by\text{-}products \end{bmatrix}$$

subject to:

MATERIAL BALANCE CONSTRAINTS ON FINAL PRODUCTS

$$(3.30) \quad \sum_{p\epsilon P} a_{cpi} z_{pi} \geq \sum_{j\epsilon J} x_{cij} + \sum_{l\epsilon L} e_{cil}. \qquad \begin{matrix} c \epsilon CF \\ i \epsilon I \end{matrix}$$

The production of final goods must at least equal the sum of shipments of final goods and exports of final goods to all markets.

MATERIAL BALANCE CONSTRAINTS ON INTERMEDIATE PRODUCTS

$$(3.31) \quad \sum_{p\epsilon P} a_{cpi} z_{pi} + \sum_{\substack{i'\epsilon I \\ i'\neq i}} x_{ci'i} + v_{ci}$$

$$\geq \sum_{\substack{i'\epsilon I \\ i'\neq i}} x_{cii'} + \sum_{l\epsilon L} e_{cil} + w_{ci}. \qquad \begin{matrix} c \epsilon CI \\ i \epsilon I \end{matrix}$$

The production of intermediate products at plant i, augmented by shipments of intermediates from other plants and imports must at least be equal to the sum of shipments of intermediate products from the ith plant to other plants, exports of intermediate products from plant i, and sales of by-products from plant i. The qualification $i' \neq i$ in the summation symbol refers to the exclusion of all shipments x of commodity c *within* a plant.

MATERIAL BALANCE CONSTRAINTS ON RAW MATERIALS AND LABOR

$$(3.32) \qquad \sum_{p \epsilon P} a_{cpi} z_{pi} + u_{ci} + v_{ci} \geq 0. \qquad\qquad \begin{matrix} c \epsilon CR \\ i \epsilon I \end{matrix}$$

Requirements for raw materials and labor for the production of intermediate and final goods c can be either purchased domestically or imported. Exports of raw materials do not explicitly enter the model, unless such exports directly compete with their domestic use. Labor requirements are met by hiring a sufficient amount of domestic labor. Imports from abroad of certain labor categories are permitted as well.

CAPACITY CONSTRAINTS

$$(3.33) \qquad \sum_{p \epsilon P} b_{mpi} z_{pi} \leq k_{mi} \qquad\qquad \begin{matrix} m \epsilon M \\ i \epsilon I \end{matrix}$$

Capacity requirements of each productive unit cannot exceed available capacity.

MARKET REQUIREMENTS

$$(3.34) \qquad \sum_{i \epsilon I} x_{cij} + v_{cj} \geq d_{cj} \qquad\qquad \begin{matrix} c \epsilon CF \\ j \epsilon J \end{matrix}$$

The shipments of final products c from all plants i to all marketing centers j, plus the imports of final product c to all marketing centers j should be sufficient to meet market requirements for each commodity c in each marketing center j.

EXPORT BOUNDS

$$(3.35) \qquad \sum_{i \epsilon I} e_{cil} \leq \bar{e}_{cl} \qquad\qquad \begin{matrix} c \epsilon (CI \cup CF) \\ l \epsilon L \end{matrix}$$

Limitations are added for the exports of intermediate and final products in order to keep such exports within realistic ranges.

NONNEGATIVITY CONSTRAINTS

$$(3.36) \qquad z_{pi}, x_{cij}, x_{cii'}, e_{cil}, v_{ci}, v_{cj}, n_{ci}, d_{ci} \geq 0 \qquad\qquad \begin{matrix} p \epsilon P \\ i \epsilon I \\ c \epsilon C \\ j \epsilon J \\ l \epsilon L \end{matrix}$$

This set of constraints is included to prevent any of the above variables from assuming a negative value.

This concludes the description of a process model with interplant shipments, exports, and imports. The full model—that is, a multi-product, dynamic process model with investment activities—can now be described.

A Multiperiod Model with Investment

At any stage in the development above, a time subscript could have been added to all the variables and coefficients, and a discount factor attached. The essential element of the dynamics, however, enters only when investment activities are introduced, because it is these activities that link the time periods together via the fact that an investment project installed in any time period will also be available for use in a number of subsequent time periods.

Economies of scale

Economies of scale in investment cost are modeled here through a linear approximation to a nonlinear cost function. Consider the investment (capital) cost function $\phi_k = f(h)$ shown in figure 2. Here the total investment costs rise with the size h of the unit installed, but at a decreasing rate so that the marginal cost of each increment of capacity is declining. This cost function often takes the form of a constant elasticity cost function; that is:

$$(3.37) \qquad \phi_\kappa = \alpha h^\beta,$$

where the exponent β represents the constant elasticity. As empirical studies have shown, β is in many cases in the range of 0.6 to 0.8. The true investment cost function $f(h)$ is approximated by the fixed-cost plus linear segment function $\hat{f}(h)$. This approximation can be written:

$$(3.38) \qquad \hat{\phi}_\kappa = \omega y + vh,$$

where

$\hat{\phi}_\kappa$ = approximate capital cost for a productive unit of size h,

ω = fixed-charge portion of investment cost,

y = 0–1 fixed-charge variable,

Figure 2. The Investment Cost Function

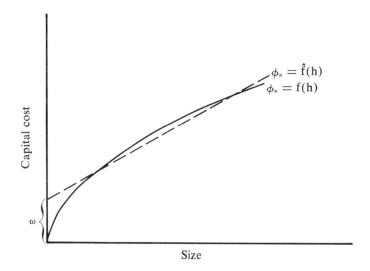

v = slope of linear portion of investment cost function,
h = size of productive unit to be installed.

If no investment is made, then y and h are both 0, and no cost is incurred. If any capacity is added, however, so that h is greater than 0, then y must be 1, and the full fixed charge must be incurred. The mechanism that forces y to assume the appropriate value will be described later. The best linear approximation to the nonlinear investment cost function depends on the capacity range that is appropriate for the planning problem at hand. Inspection of figure 2 makes clear that the wider the relevant capacity range, the higher the fixed charge ω and the smaller the slope v of the linear approximation that provides the closest fit to the original investment cost function.

If all capital costs for a given period were charged in the period the project was installed, the timing of investments that the model would recommend would be distorted. Clearly, investment in the latter part of the planning period would be discouraged because the capacity installed is likely to generate greater costs than the benefits observed during the planning period. Also, this treatment of capital costs would represent a poor representation of reality, because investments are normally financed from loans that are periodically repaid. To con-

vert the capital costs associated with capacity expansion in the model
to an even stream of payments that are sufficient to cover the original
cost plus interest charges for the productive unit over the period of
its useful life, a capital recovery factor is applied to each investment.[2]
The capital recovery factor for productive unit m can be written as:

(3.39)
$$\sigma_m = \frac{\rho(1 + \rho)^{\varsigma_m}}{(1 + \rho)^{\varsigma_m} - 1}$$

$$= \frac{\rho}{1 - (1 + \rho)^{-\varsigma_m}},$$

which is the familiar formula for computing an annuity with present
value equal to 1, where

σ_m = capital recovery factor,
ρ = discount rate per time interval,
ς_m = useful life of productive unit m.

In an appendix to this chapter, a full derivation of the capital recovery factor is given, as well as a number of typical values of the
capital recovery factor for different discount rates and plant and
equipment lifetimes.

Applying the capital recovery factor to the investment cost approximation, we obtain the periodical investment charge on a capacity
increase for productive unit m at plant i as:

$$\sigma_m(\omega_m y_m + \nu_m h_m).$$

The model should not begin to incur this periodical investment
charge (which may also be interpreted as a rental payment) on an
investment until the period in which the project is installed, but it
should incur the rental in each time period after the unit is placed
in operation. This is accomplished by computing the capital cost for
each time period as follows:

(3.40) $$\phi_{\kappa t} = \sum_{\tau=1}^{t} \sum_{i \in I} \sum_{m \in M} \sigma_m (\omega_{mi\tau} y_{mi\tau} + \nu_{mi\tau} h_{mi\tau}),$$

2. See chapter 2, footnote 3 for a discussion of at least one circumstance in
which a different treatment of capital costs should be used.

where

$\phi_{\kappa t}$ = the capital charges incurred in each period,

σ_m = capital recovery factor for productive unit m,

$\omega_{mi\tau}$ = fixed charge for investment in productive unit m at plant i in period τ,

$y_{mi\tau}$ = 0–1 investment variable for productive unit m at plant i in period τ,

$v_{mi\tau}$ = linear portion of investment cost for productive unit m at plant i in period τ,

$h_{mi\tau}$ = size of new productive unit m installed at plant i in period τ.

To see exactly how this works, consider an example of a steel shop. In period 1 no capacity is added. In period 2 a new BOF converter is installed with a capacity of 200,000 metric tons of steel a year. In period 3 no new capacity is installed. In this case, in which subscripts refer to time:

$$y_1 = 0, \qquad h_1 = \quad 0;$$
$$y_2 = 1, \qquad h_2 = 200;$$
$$y_3 = 0, \qquad h_3 = \quad 0.$$

Dropping the m and i subscripts on (3.40), since a single productive unit and plant are being considered, (3.40) can be rewritten as:

(3.41)
$$\phi_{\kappa t} = \sum_{\tau=1}^{t} \sigma(\omega_\tau y_\tau + v_\tau h_\tau).$$

Then, for time periods 1, 2, and 3:

$$\phi_{\kappa 1} = \sigma(\omega_1 y_1 + v_1 h_1) = 0,$$

$$\phi_{\kappa 2} = \sigma(\omega_1 y_1 + v_1 h_1 + \omega_2 y_2 + v_2 h_2) = \sigma(\omega_2 + 200\, v_2),$$

$$\phi_{\kappa 3} = \sigma(\omega_1 y_1 + v_1 h_1 + \omega_2 y_2 + v_2 h_2 + \omega_3 y_3 + v_3 h_3)$$

$$= \sigma(\omega_2 + 200\, v_2).$$

Thus, in both period 2 and period 3, the model incurs rental charges on the new capacity installed in period 2, but no payment is made in period 1.

This specification also results in the modification of the capacity constraint from the form (3.33) used in the previous model to:

$$(3.42) \qquad \sum_{p \epsilon P} b_{mpi} z_{pit} \leq k_{mi} + \sum_{\substack{\tau \epsilon T \\ \tau \leq t}} (h_{mi\tau} - s_{mi\tau}), \qquad \begin{array}{l} m \epsilon M \\ i \epsilon I \\ \tau, t \epsilon T \end{array}$$

where

$s_{mi\tau}$ = expected retirement of capacity in productive unit m at plant i in time period τ,

k_{mi} = initial capacity of productive unit m at plant i.

The s variables are chosen exogenously to the model. For example, if the productive unit m were the steel shop, the initial capacity might include a number of open hearth furnaces that were slated for retirement during the period covered by the model. Then $s_{mi\tau}$ would represent the capacity to be retired in each time period τ. The effect of the summation over τ for τ less than or equal to t in (3.42) is to permit all capacity installed in previous periods to be available for use in period t.

Two additional constraints are needed to complete the specification of investment in the model. These two constraints introduce directly into the model the side condition:

$$y = 0 \text{ when } h = 0,$$
$$y = 1 \text{ when } h > 0,$$

which was used in specifying the approximation to the investment cost function. These constraints are:

$$(3.43) \qquad \qquad h_{mit} \leq \bar{h}_{mit} y_{mit}, \qquad \qquad \begin{array}{l} m \epsilon M \\ i \epsilon I \\ t \epsilon T \end{array}$$

and

$$(3.44) \qquad \qquad y_{mit} = 0 \text{ or } 1, \qquad \qquad \begin{array}{l} m \epsilon M \\ i \epsilon I \\ t \epsilon T \end{array}$$

where

$\bar{h}_{mit}$ = an upper bound on the size of capacity unit that can be added to productive unit m at plant i in period t

T = the set of time periods covered by the model.

Figure 3.   Investment Cost Function with Diseconomies of Scale

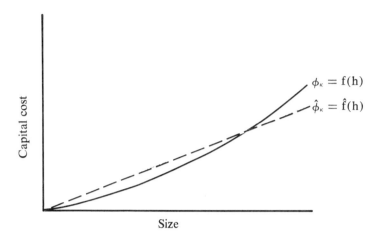

The effect of (3.43) and (3.44) is to prohibit any addition to capacity unless the fixed charge is incurred, and the fixed charge is only incurred if y_{mit} is equal to 1. From (3.43) it follows that y_{mit} must be placed at 1 if h_{mit} is positive for the constraint to hold. If h_{mit} is 0, y_{mit} will be forced to 0 by the model as the cost minimization objective of the model leads to a preference for not incurring the fixed charge.

Diseconomies of scale

If the investment cost function in figure 2 is characterized by diseconomies rather than by economies of scale, the problem becomes an ordinary linear program rather than a mixed-integer program and is therefore greatly simplified. Such a function, and its approximation, are shown in figure 3.

In this case the integer variable, y, is not needed, and the function can be approximated simply as:

$$(3.45) \qquad \hat{\phi}_\kappa = vh .$$

If a closer approximation is desired, a piecewise linear approximation with several segments can be constructed, as shown in figure 4. This approximation is made by defining new variables h_1, h_2, and so on, such that:

Figure 4.   A Piecewise Linear Approximation to an Investment Cost Function with Diseconomies of Scale

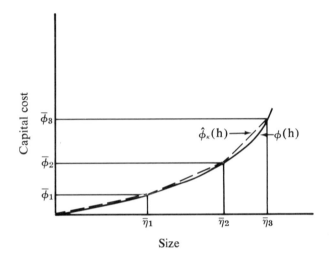

(3.46) $$h = h_1 + h_2 + h_3 \, ,$$

with

(3.47) $$h_i \leq \bar{\eta}_{i+1} - \bar{\eta}_i \, ,$$

and with

(3.48) $$\hat{\phi}(h) = \sum_i \nu_i h_i \, ,$$

where

(3.49) $$\nu_i = \frac{\bar{\phi}_{i+1} - \bar{\phi}_i}{\bar{\eta}_{i+1} - \bar{\eta}_i} \, ,$$

and

(3.50) $$\bar{\phi}_i = f(\bar{\eta}_i).$$

The procedure used here is to choose a set of grid fixed points $\bar{\eta}_i$ that provide a satisfactory approximation. The true cost function f in (3.50) is then used to map each grid point $\bar{\eta}_i$ to the related capital cost $\bar{\phi}_i$. Next, the $\bar{\eta}$ and $\bar{\phi}$ points are used to calculate the slopes ν_i with (3.49). Finally, h is replaced whenever it occurs in the problem by equation (3.46); $\hat{\phi}(h)$ is replaced with (3.48); and the additional constraint (3.47) is added to the problem. This procedure can be used only in the presence of diseconomies of scale.

Two Further Modifications

Two additional modifications should be noted before the complete model is stated in the next chapter. The first is a more detailed break-down of raw material and labor inputs; the second is the specification of the discounting procedure.

Raw materials and labor inputs

$$(3.51) \qquad \sum_{p \in P} a_{cpi} z_{pi} + u_{ci} + v_{ci} \geq 0. \qquad \begin{matrix} c \in CR \\ i \in I \end{matrix}$$

All raw materials and labor can be either purchased domestically or imported. Frequently, the import price for certain commodities will be substantially higher than the domestic price or vice versa, so it is possible to divide the set of raw materials into three groups: those which will be purchased domestically, those which will be imported, and those which will be either purchased domestically or imported. For example, in many cases fuel oil will be an imported commodity and labor will be a domestically hired input. The advantage of this partitioning of the set of raw material and labor inputs will be shown later when this specification is used to reduce the number of con-straints in the model. Thus, one must partition the set CR into the sets:

CRD = raw materials and labor input that are purchased domestically;

CRI = raw materials and labor inputs that are imported;

$CRDI$ = raw materials and labor inputs that may be either imported or purchased domestically.

The discounting procedure

The discounting procedure would be straightforward except for the fact that each time period in investment planning models normally includes several years. Consider, for example, a model that covers a nine-year interval, has annual time periods, and has a cost ϕ_t in each year. The discounted cost for the first year would be $(1 + \rho)^{-1}\phi_t$; for the second year, $(1 + \rho)^{-2}\phi_t$; and for the entire period:

(3.52) $$\xi = \sum_{\tau=1}^{9} (1 + \rho)^{-\tau}\phi_\tau ,$$

where

ρ = the annual discount rate.

If, however, this specification made the model too large to solve, as all constraints should now be specified annually, it might be necessary to specify it as a model with three time periods of three years' duration each. This would reduce the number of constraints by approximately two-thirds. The cost charges for each time period would now be:

$$\begin{aligned}
\psi_1 &= \phi_\tau, & \tau &= 1, 2, 3, \\
\psi_2 &= \phi_\tau, & \tau &= 4, 5, 6, \\
\psi_3 &= \phi_\tau, & \tau &= 7, 8, 9,
\end{aligned}$$

where

ψ_t is the average annual cost for each year during time period t.

Then, (3.52) can be written as:

(3.53)

$$\xi = \psi_1 \sum_{\tau=1}^{3} (1 + \rho)^{-\tau} + \psi_2 \sum_{\tau=4}^{6} (1 + \rho)^{-\tau} + \psi_3 \sum_{\tau=7}^{9} (1 + \rho)^{-\tau},$$

where the first term on the right-hand side of (3.53) is the discounted sum of the investment charges during the first three-year period, the second term is the discounted sum of such charges for the second three-year period, and so forth. Equation (3.53) can now be rewritten as:

$$\xi = \sum_{\tau=1}^{3} \delta_t \psi_t,$$

where

$$\delta_t = \sum_{\tau=3(t-1)+1}^{3(t-1)+3} (1 + \rho)^{-\tau}$$

$$= \sum_{\tau=1}^{3} (1 + \rho)^{-3(t-1)-\tau}.$$

For example, for the first three-year period, δ_1 is equal to:

$$\sum_{\tau=1}^{3} (1 + \rho)^{-3(t-1)-\tau} = \sum_{\tau=1}^{3} (1 + \rho)^{-\tau},$$

as in (3.53). The general form of (3.53) can now be written as:

(3.54)
$$\delta_t = \sum_{\tau=1}^{\theta} (1 + \rho)^{-\theta(t-1)-\tau},$$

where

$\theta =$ the number of years per time period.

By incorporating the investment constraints and activities into the process model, a model for project selection under economies of scale can be constructed. This is done in chapter 4.

Appendix. The Capital Recovery Factor

This appendix presents the complete derivation of the capital recovery factor (CRF). The CRF is defined as the factor that converts the capital costs associated with capacity construction to an even stream of payments that are sufficient to repay the original capital costs augmented by interest charges over the period of the useful life of the productive unit. Let:

ϕ_κ = total construction cost,
$\phi_{\kappa t}$ = annual construction cost charge,
ρ = discount rate,
ζ_m = life of productive unit m,
η = principal outstanding,
σ_m = capital recovery factor for productive unit m.

If $\rho = 0$, then $\sigma_m = 1/\zeta_m$, and $\phi_{\kappa t} = \phi_\kappa/\zeta_m$. If $\rho \neq 0$, then the CRF is derived in the following way: it is assumed that payments of equal amounts are made at the end of each time interval, and that the entire capital outlay is made at the beginning of the year in which construction of capacity is begun.

$$\eta_0 = \phi_\kappa,$$

$$\eta_1 = \eta_0 (1 + \rho) - \phi_{\kappa t},$$

.

.

.

.

$$\eta_i = \eta_{i-1} (1 + \rho) - \phi_{\kappa t},$$

.

.

.

.

$$\eta_{\zeta m} = \eta_{\zeta_m - 1} (1 + \rho) - \phi_{\kappa t} = 0.$$

Therefore,

$$\eta_{\zeta m} = \eta_0 (1 + \rho)^{\zeta m} - \phi_{\kappa t} \sum_{i=1}^{\zeta m} (1 + \rho)^{i-1} = 0.$$

Solving the above for $\phi_{\kappa t}$ yields:

(3.i)
$$\phi_{\kappa t} = \frac{\eta_0 (1 + \rho)^{\zeta m}}{\displaystyle\sum_{i=1}^{\zeta m} (1 + \rho)^{i-1}}.$$

Now, consider only the denominator of the right-hand side of this expression and define:

(3.ii) $\displaystyle S = \sum_{i=1}^{\zeta m} (1 + \rho)^{i-1}$

$$= 1 + (1 + \rho) + (1 + \rho)^2 + \cdots + (1 + \rho)^{\zeta m - 1} ;$$

then:

(3.iii) $\quad (1 + \rho) S = (1 + \rho) + (1 + \rho)^2 + (1 + \rho)^3 + \cdots$

$$+ (1 + \rho)^{\zeta m}.$$

So, subtraction of (3.iii) from (3.ii) yields:

$$[1 - (1 + \rho)] S = 1 - (1 + \rho)^{\zeta_m},$$

or

(3.iv)
$$S = \frac{1 - (1 + \rho)^{\zeta_m}}{-\rho}.$$

Substitution of (3.iv) into (3.i) and the use of $\eta_0 = \phi_\kappa$ gives:

(3.v)
$$\phi_{\kappa t} = \frac{\phi_k (1 + \rho)^{\zeta_m} (-\rho)}{1 - (1 + \rho)^{\zeta_m}}$$

$$= \frac{-\phi_\kappa \rho}{(1 + \rho)^{-\zeta_m} - 1},$$

or

(3.vi)
$$\phi_{\kappa t} = \frac{\phi_\kappa \rho}{1 - (1 + \rho)^{-\zeta_m}},$$

$$\sigma_m = \frac{\rho}{1 - (1 + \rho)^{-\zeta_m}}$$

$$= \frac{\rho (1 + \rho)^{\zeta_m}}{(1 + \rho)^{\zeta_m} - 1}.$$

Table 1 contains some typical values for the CRF depending on the interest rate ρ, the lifetime of the capacity ζ_m, and assuming annual payments at the end of each year.

Table 1. Typical Values for Capital Recovery Factors

Capacity lifetime, ζ_m	$\rho = 0.05$	$\rho = 0.10$	$\rho = 0.15$
10	0.1295	0.1627	0.1993
11	0.1204	0.1540	0.1911
12	0.1128	0.1468	0.1845
13	0.1065	0.1408	0.1791
14	0.1010	0.1357	0.1747
15	0.0963	0.1315	0.1710
20	0.0802	0.1175	0.1598
25	0.0710	0.1102	0.1547
30	0.0651	0.1061	0.1523

4

A Model for Project Selection

IN THE MULTIPERIOD PROJECT SELECTION MODEL, one seeks to find the minimum discounted cost of meeting specified market requirements over the period covered by the model. This search involves the selection of activity levels for the following variables:

- increments to capacity;
- shipments from plants to markets and among plants;
- imports;
- exports;
- domestic purchases of raw materials, miscellaneous material inputs, and labor; and
- by-product sales.

The complete model can now be described. This is done by first presenting all of the symbols used in the model, followed by a statement of the constraints and criterion function. Next, the size of the model will be considered. Since each project selection situation is different and none can be expected to conform to any standard complete model, two procedures for altering the model are suggested. First, a number of the principal variants of the complete model are described; then, a LEGO set of alternative model parts is provided along with instructions on how to construct a "do-it-yourself" model.[1]

---

1. LEGO is the brand name for a type of interlocking children's building blocks.

The Complete Model

The symbols used in the model can be categorized as the sets and indexes, the variables, and the parameters, as follows:

Symbol	*Definition*
THE SETS AND INDEXES	
$i, i' \epsilon I$	Plant sites
$j \epsilon J$	Domestic market areas
$l \epsilon L$	Export market areas
$m \epsilon M$	Productive units
$p \epsilon P$	Production processes
$\tau, t \epsilon T$	Time intervals and time periods
$c \epsilon C$	Commodities used or produced in the industry
CF	Final products of the industry
CI	Intermediate products
CR	Raw materials, miscellaneous inputs, and labor
THE VARIABLES	
z	Process levels (production levels)
x	Domestic shipments
e	Exports
v	Imports
u	Domestic purchases
w	Domestic sales of by-products
y	0–1 investment decisions
h	Continuous investment decisions
ϕ	Cost groups
κ	Capital costs
ψ	Recurrent costs
λ	Transportation costs
ξ	Total costs
π	Import costs
ϵ	Export revenues
χ	Domestic sales
THE PARAMETERS	
a	Process inputs ($-$) or outputs ($+$)
b	Capacity utilization
k	Initial capacity
s	Retirements of capacity

Symbol	Definition
d	Market requirements
$\bar{e}$	Export bounds
$\bar{h}$	Maximum capacity expansion per time period
Θ	Number of time intervals per time period
ρ	Discount rate per time interval
δ	Discount factor
σ_m	Capital recovery factor for productive unit m
σ_m	$\dfrac{\rho(1+\rho)^{\zeta_m}}{(1+\rho)^{\zeta_m}-1}$, where ζ_m = life of productive unit m
ω	Fixed-charge portion of investment costs
ν	Linear portion of investment costs
β	Recurrent costs related to capacity
p	Prices
μ	Unit transportation costs

The constraints of the model are as follows:

MATERIAL BALANCE CONSTRAINTS ON FINAL PRODUCTS

$$(4.1) \quad \sum_{p\epsilon P} a_{cpi}\, z_{pit} \geq \sum_{j\epsilon J} x_{cijt} + \sum_{l\epsilon L} e_{cilt} \qquad\qquad \begin{array}{l} c\,\epsilon\,CF \\ i\,\epsilon\,I \\ t\,\epsilon\,T \end{array}$$

$$\begin{bmatrix} Output\ of \\ final\ products \end{bmatrix} \geq \begin{bmatrix} Domestic \\ shipments \\ of\ final \\ products \end{bmatrix} + \begin{bmatrix} Exports\ of \\ final \\ products \end{bmatrix}$$

MATERIAL BALANCE CONSTRAINTS ON INTERMEDIATE PRODUCTS

$$(4.2) \quad \sum_{p\epsilon P} a_{cpi}\, z_{pit} + \sum_{\substack{i'\neq i \\ i'\epsilon I}} x_{ci'it} + v_{cit}$$

$$\begin{bmatrix} Output\ of \\ intermediate \\ products\ at \\ plant\ i \end{bmatrix} + \begin{bmatrix} Shipments\ of \\ intermediate \\ products\ from \\ plant\ i'\ to \\ plant\ i \end{bmatrix} + \begin{bmatrix} Imports\ of \\ intermediate \\ products\ to \\ plant\ i \end{bmatrix}$$

$$\geq \sum_{\substack{i'\neq i \\ i'\epsilon I}} x_{cii't} + \sum_{l\epsilon L} e_{cilt} + w_{cit} \qquad\qquad \begin{array}{l} c\,\epsilon\,CI \\ i\,\epsilon\,I \\ t\,\epsilon\,T \end{array}$$

$$\geq \begin{bmatrix} Shipments\ of \\ intermediate \\ products \\ from\ plant\ i \\ to\ plant\ i' \end{bmatrix} + \begin{bmatrix} Exports\ of \\ intermediate \\ products \\ from\ plant\ i \end{bmatrix} + \begin{bmatrix} Domestic\ sales \\ of\ by\text{-}products \\ from\ plant\ i \end{bmatrix}$$

MATERIAL BALANCE CONSTRAINTS ON RAW MATERIALS AND LABOR INPUTS

$$(4.3) \quad \sum_{p \epsilon P} a_{cpi} z_{pit} + u_{cit} + v_{cit} \geq 0 \qquad\qquad c \epsilon CR$$
$$i \epsilon I$$
$$t \epsilon T$$

$$\begin{bmatrix} Use\ of\ domestic \\ or\ imported\ raw \\ materials\ and \\ labor \end{bmatrix} + \begin{bmatrix} Local\ raw \\ materials \\ and\ labor \end{bmatrix} + \begin{bmatrix} Imported\ raw \\ materials\ and \\ labor \end{bmatrix} \geq 0$$

CAPACITY CONSTRAINTS

$$(4.4) \quad \sum_{p \epsilon P} b_{mpi} z_{pit} \leq k_{mi} + \sum_{\substack{\tau \epsilon T \\ \tau \leq t}} (h_{mi\tau} - s_{mi\tau}) \qquad\qquad m \epsilon M$$
$$i \epsilon I$$
$$\tau, t \epsilon T$$

$$\begin{bmatrix} Capacity \\ required \end{bmatrix} \leq \begin{bmatrix} Initial \\ capacity \end{bmatrix} + \begin{bmatrix} Capacity \\ expansion \end{bmatrix} - \begin{bmatrix} Capacity \\ retirements \end{bmatrix}$$

MARKET REQUIREMENTS

$$(4.5) \quad \sum_{i \epsilon I} x_{cijt} + v_{cjt} \geq d_{cjt} \qquad\qquad c \epsilon CF$$
$$j \epsilon J$$
$$t \epsilon T$$

$$\begin{bmatrix} Domestic \\ shipments \end{bmatrix} + [Imports] \geq \begin{bmatrix} Market \\ requirements \end{bmatrix}$$

EXPORT CONSTRAINTS

$$(4.6) \quad \sum_{i \epsilon I} e_{cilt} \leq \bar{e}_{clt} \qquad\qquad c \epsilon (CI \cup CF)$$
$$l \epsilon L$$
$$t \epsilon T$$

$$\begin{bmatrix} Export\ of \\ commodity\ c \end{bmatrix} \leq \begin{bmatrix} Upper\ bounds\ on \\ exports \end{bmatrix}$$

INVESTMENT CONSTRAINTS ON MAXIMUM INVESTMENT

$$(4.7) \quad h_{mit} \leq \bar{h}_{mit} y_{mit} \qquad\qquad m \epsilon M$$
$$i \epsilon I$$
$$t \epsilon T$$

$$\begin{bmatrix} Increment\ to \\ capacity \end{bmatrix} \leq \begin{bmatrix} Upper\ bound \\ on\ increment \\ to\ capacity \end{bmatrix} \begin{bmatrix} 0\text{--}1 \\ investment \\ variable \end{bmatrix}$$

INVESTMENT CONSTRAINTS ON 0–1 INVESTMENT

$$(4.8) \quad y_{mit} = 0 \text{ or } 1 \qquad\qquad m \epsilon M$$
$$i \epsilon I$$
$$t \epsilon T$$

NONNEGATIVITY CONSTRAINTS

(4.9)

$$z_{pit} \geq 0 \qquad\qquad\qquad p \epsilon P,\ i \epsilon I,\ t \epsilon T$$

$$x_{cijt} \geq 0 \qquad c \epsilon CF, \qquad j \epsilon J,\ i \epsilon I,\ t \epsilon T$$

$$x_{cii't} \geq 0 \qquad c \epsilon CI, \qquad i' \epsilon I,\ i \epsilon I,\ t \epsilon T$$
$$\qquad\qquad\qquad\qquad\qquad\qquad i' \neq i$$

$$v_{cit} \geq 0 \qquad c \epsilon CR, \qquad\qquad i \epsilon I,\ t \epsilon T$$

$$e_{cilt} \geq 0 \qquad c \epsilon (CI \cup CF),\ l \epsilon L,\ i \epsilon I,\ t \epsilon T$$

$$w_{cit} \geq 0 \qquad c \epsilon CI, \qquad\qquad i \epsilon I,\ t \epsilon T$$

$$u_{cit} \geq 0 \qquad c \epsilon CR, \qquad\qquad i \epsilon I,\ t \epsilon T$$

$$h_{mit} \geq 0 \qquad\qquad\qquad m \epsilon M,\ i \epsilon I,\ t \epsilon T$$

$$y_{mit} \geq 0 \qquad\qquad\qquad m \epsilon M,\ i \epsilon I,\ t \epsilon T$$

$$v_{cjt} \geq 0 \qquad c \epsilon CF. \qquad\qquad j \epsilon J,\ t \epsilon T$$

These constraints must be satisfied while seeking to minimize the discounted costs of production, transport, and investment specified as follows:

(4.10) $\quad \xi = \sum\limits_{t \epsilon T} \delta_t(\phi_{\kappa t} + \phi_{\psi t} + \phi_{\lambda t} + \phi_{\pi t} - \phi_{\epsilon t} - \phi_{\chi t}),$

$$\begin{bmatrix} Total \\ costs \end{bmatrix} = \begin{bmatrix} Capital \\ costs \end{bmatrix} + \begin{bmatrix} Recurrent \\ costs \end{bmatrix} + \begin{bmatrix} Transport \\ costs \end{bmatrix}$$
$$+ \begin{bmatrix} Import \\ costs \end{bmatrix} - \begin{bmatrix} Export \\ revenues \end{bmatrix} - \begin{bmatrix} Sales\ of \\ by\text{-}products \end{bmatrix}$$

where

$$\delta_t = \sum\limits_{\gamma=1}^{\theta} (1 + \rho)^{-\theta(t-1)-\gamma},$$

[*Discount factor*]

$\theta = $ number of time intervals per time period;

(4.11) $\quad \phi_{\kappa t} = \sum\limits_{\tau=1}^{t} \sum\limits_{i \epsilon I} \sum\limits_{m \epsilon M} \sigma_m \left(\omega_{mi\tau}\, y_{mi\tau} + v_{mi\tau}\, h_{mi\tau} \right);$

$$\begin{bmatrix} Capital \\ costs \end{bmatrix} = \begin{bmatrix} Fixed \\ charge \end{bmatrix} + \begin{bmatrix} Linear\ portion \\ of\ capital\ costs \end{bmatrix}$$

(4.12) $\quad \phi_{\psi t} = \sum\limits_{\tau=1}^{t} \sum\limits_{i \epsilon I} \sum\limits_{m \epsilon M} \beta_{mi\tau}\, h_{mi\tau} + \sum\limits_{c \epsilon CR} \sum\limits_{i \epsilon I} p^d_{cit}\, u_{cit} ;$

$$\begin{bmatrix} Recurrent \\ costs \end{bmatrix} = \begin{bmatrix} Recurrent\ costs \\ related\ to\ capacity \end{bmatrix} + \begin{bmatrix} Local\ raw \\ materials\ and \\ labor\ costs \end{bmatrix}$$

(4.13) $\phi_{\lambda t} = \sum\limits_{c \epsilon CF} (\sum\limits_{i \epsilon I} \sum\limits_{j \epsilon J} \mu_{cijt}\, x_{cijt} + \sum\limits_{i \epsilon I} \mu_{cjt}\, v_{cjt} + \sum\limits_{i \epsilon I} \sum\limits_{l \epsilon L} \mu_{cilt}\, e_{cilt})$

$$\begin{bmatrix} Transport \\ costs \end{bmatrix} = \begin{bmatrix} Final \\ products \end{bmatrix} [Domestic + Imported + Exported]$$

$+ \sum\limits_{c \epsilon CI} (\sum\limits_{i \epsilon I} \sum\limits_{\substack{i' \epsilon I \\ i' \neq i}} \mu_{cii't}\, x_{cii't} + \sum\limits_{i \epsilon I} \mu_{cit}\, v_{cit} + \sum\limits_{i \epsilon I} \sum\limits_{e \epsilon L} \mu_{cilt}\, e_{cilt})$

$+ \begin{bmatrix} Intermediate \\ products \end{bmatrix} [Interplant + Imports + Exports]$

$+ \sum\limits_{c \epsilon CR} (\sum\limits_{i \epsilon I} \mu_{cit}\, v_{cit})\,;$

$+ \begin{bmatrix} Raw\ materials \\ and\ labor \end{bmatrix} [Imports]$

(4.14) $\phi_{\pi t} = \sum\limits_{c \epsilon CF} \sum\limits_{j \epsilon J} p^{v}_{cjt}\, v_{cjt} + \sum\limits_{c \epsilon (CI\ \cup\ CR)} \sum\limits_{i \epsilon I} p^{v}_{cit}\, v_{cit}\,;$

$$\begin{bmatrix} Import \\ costs \end{bmatrix} = \begin{bmatrix} Final\ product \\ imports \end{bmatrix} + \begin{bmatrix} Intermediate,\ raw\ materials, \\ and\ labor\ imports \end{bmatrix}$$

(4.15) $\phi_{\epsilon t} = \sum\limits_{c \epsilon (CF\ \cup\ CI)} \sum\limits_{i \epsilon I} \sum\limits_{l \epsilon L} p^{e}_{cilt}\, e_{cilt}\,;$

$$\begin{bmatrix} Export \\ revenues \end{bmatrix} = \begin{bmatrix} Final\ and\ intermediate \\ product\ export\ revenues \end{bmatrix}$$

(4.16) $\phi_{\chi t} = \sum\limits_{c \epsilon CI} \sum\limits_{i \epsilon I} p^{d}_{cit}\, w_{cit}\,.$

$$\begin{bmatrix} Domestic\ sales \\ revenue\ of \\ by\text{-}products \end{bmatrix} = \begin{bmatrix} Domestic\ sales \\ revenue\ of \\ by\text{-}products \end{bmatrix}$$

All parts but one of this model have been discussed earlier. The one addition is the β parameter in equality (4.12). This parameter represents the portion of recurrent costs that is not proportional to actual production levels but rather to the capacity installed. Examples are the maintenance costs and insurance payments on any piece of capital equipment.

Size of the Model

Before beginning any analysis of a project selection problem, we must point out the size of the resulting computational problem. In the original formulation of the problem, it is frequently disaggregated into more markets, plants, productive units, and time periods than present-day computers can handle. In order to permit calculation of model size, it is essential first to develop some notation. The notation here can be simplified if the reader will permit momentarily the use of a symbol for a set to define the number of elements in that set. For example, we shall use J not to represent the set of markets but rather the number of markets. With this license, the number of elements in the model above may be written as:

CONSTRAINTS

Relation	*Number*
(4.1)	$CF.I.T$
(4.2)	$CI.I.T$
(4.3)	$CRD.I.T$
(4.4)	$CRI.I.T$
(4.5)	$CRDI.I.T$
(4.6)	$M.I.T$
(4.7)	$CF.J.T$
(4.8)	$(CI + CF).L.T.$
(4.9)	$M.I.T.$

$$C.I.T + 2.M.I.T + CF.J.T + (CI + CF).L.T$$
$$\text{or } [(C + 2.M).I.T + CF.J + (CI + CF).L].T$$

VARIABLES

Variable	*Number*
z_{pit}	$P.I.T$
x_{cijt}	$CF.J.I.T$
$x_{cii't}$	$CI.(I - 1).I.T$
v_{cit}	$(CRD + CRDI).I.T$
e_{cilt}	$(CI + CF).L.I.T$
w_{cit}	$CI.I.T$
u_{cit}	$CR.I.T$
h_{mit}	$M.I.T$
y_{mit}	$M.I.T$
v_{cjt}	$CF.J.T$

$$[\{P + CF.J + CI\,(I - 1) + (CRI + CRDI) + CI + CF)L$$
$$+ CI + CRD + 2M\}I + CF.J]T$$
or, using $CR = CRI + CRDI + CRD,$
$$[\{P + CF.J + CI(I = 1) + CR + (CI + CF)L$$
$$+ CI + 2M\} I + CF.J]T$$

In summary:

$$\text{constraints} = [(C + 2M)I + CF.J + (CI + CF)L]T,$$
$$\text{variables} = [\{(P + CF.J + CI(I - 1) + CR$$
$$+ (CI + CF)L + CI + 2M\} I + CF.J]T,$$
$$\text{integer variables} = M.I.T,$$

where

    C = commodities = $CF \cup CI \cup CRD \cup CRI \cup CRDI,$
  CF = final commodities,
  CI = intermediate commodities,
  CR = raw materials, miscellaneous inputs, and labor =
        $CRD \cup CRI \cup CRDI,$
    M = productive units,
    P = processes,
    I = plant sites,
    J = markets,
    T = periods,
    L = export markets.

Consider a problem of 3 plant sites, 8 markets, 3 time periods, 10 productive units, 12 processes, and 3 export markets. Also, the problem has a breakdown of 5 final commodities, 7 intermediate commodities, and 8 raw materials, to total 20 commodities. In this case, there would be 588 constraints, no bounds, 1,354 regular variables, and 90 integer variables. That is not an unusually large linear program, and it could probably be solved in a few minutes on a large computer. The mixed-integer programming formulation with 90 integer variables, however, is a very large problem, and, though problems of this size have been solved, the analyst should not in general expect to obtain a global optimum solution to such a problem.[2] Therefore, the number of integer variables should normally be reduced to the absolute minimum number necessary before an attempt is made to solve the problem—or else the analyst should decide that in all probability he will have to be content with a local optimum solution to the model.[3]

2. The seemingly cryptic term "global optimum solution" will be explained in chapter 8.

3. Again, see chapter 8.

Variants of the Model

Two variants of the model that may prove to be particularly useful are discussed here.

Indivisible investments

In some industries, productive units are not available in all sizes but only in a small set of different sizes. In others, the size of productive units may not be at issue but rather only the question of whether or not to invest in a particular project at a certain time. Examples include LD converters in the steel industry or generators in power stations. These units are typically built in one of a few sizes that are currently being constructed.

In such cases the h variables and the investment constraints (4.7) of the complete model are dropped, and the capacity constraints (4.4) are rewritten as:

$$(4.17) \qquad \sum_{p \epsilon P} b_{mpi} z_{pit} \leq k_{mi} + \sum_{\substack{\tau \epsilon T \\ \tau \leq t}} \eta_{mi\tau} y_{mi\tau}, \qquad \begin{array}{c} m \epsilon M \\ i \epsilon I \\ t \epsilon T \end{array}$$

where

$\eta_{mi\tau}$ = capacity of the productive unit under consideration for installation in productive unit m at plant i in time period τ.

Also the h variables in the capital cost function (4.11) are dropped and the coefficient ω becomes the capital costs for the indivisible project.

Project size and time-phasing

Frequently, the issue in project selection is not the question of where investments should be made, but rather whether, when, and what size. The model above can be collapsed for such purposes by aggregating across all plants, domestic markets, and export markets.

The resulting model is to minimize[4]:

$$(4.18) \quad \xi = \sum_{t \epsilon T} \delta_t \left(\phi_{\kappa t} + \phi_{\psi t} + \phi_{\pi t} - \phi_{\epsilon t} - \phi_{\chi t} \right),$$

where

$$(4.19) \quad \phi_{\kappa t} = \sum_{\tau=1}^{t} \sum_{m \epsilon M} \sigma_m \left(\omega_{m\tau} \, y_{m\tau} + v_{m\tau} \, h_{m\tau} \right),$$

$$(4.20) \quad \phi_{\psi t} = \sum_{\tau=1}^{t} \sum_{m \epsilon M} \beta_{m\tau} \, h_{m\tau} + \sum_{c \epsilon CR} p^d{}_{ct} \, u_{ct},$$

$$(4.21) \quad \phi_{\pi t} = \sum_{c \epsilon CF} p^v{}_{ct} \, v_{ct} + \sum_{c \epsilon (CI \cup CR)} p^v{}_{ct} \, v_{ct},$$

$$(4.22) \quad \phi_{\epsilon t} = \sum_{c \epsilon (CF \cup CI)} p^e{}_{ct} \, e_{ct},$$

$$(4.23) \quad \phi_{\chi t} = \sum_{c \epsilon CI} p^d{}_{ct} \, w_{ct};$$

subject to:

MATERIAL BALANCE CONSTRAINTS ON FINAL PRODUCTS

$$(4.24) \qquad \sum_{p \epsilon P} a_{cp} \, z_{pt} \geq x_{ct} + e_{ct} \qquad\qquad \begin{array}{l} c \epsilon CF \\ t \epsilon T \end{array}$$

MATERIAL BALANCE CONSTRAINTS ON INTERMEDIATE PRODUCTS

$$(4.25) \qquad \sum_{p \epsilon P} a_{cp} \, z_{pt} + v_{ct} \geq e_{ct} + w_{ct} \qquad\qquad \begin{array}{l} c \epsilon CI \\ t \epsilon T \end{array}$$

4. If location of new investments is not considered a major issue, it is necessary to specify the reasons for this in order to decide whether or not transport costs need be considered in the model. If locational choice is disregarded because transport costs are unimportant in absolute terms or because transport cost implications of alternative locations and imports are more or less similar, then transport costs do not have to be considered explicitly in the model. If, however, locational choice can be disregarded in the model because a site has been selected a priori, then transport costs need to be considered if imports from abroad are possible, and the optimal choice between domestic production and imports is to be based on delivered cost to the marketing center. The model in this section does not incorporate transport costs; if they need to be included, the criterion function of the complete project selection model (4.10) must be used.

MATERIAL BALANCE CONSTRAINTS ON RAW MATERIALS AND LABOR

$$(4.26) \qquad \sum_{p \epsilon P} a_{cp} \, z_{pt} + u_{ct} + v_{ct} \geq 0 \qquad\qquad c \, \epsilon \, CR$$
$$t \, \epsilon \, T$$

CAPACITY CONSTRAINTS

$$(4.27) \qquad \sum_{p \epsilon P} b_{mp} \, z_{pt} \leq k_m + \sum_{\substack{\tau \epsilon T \\ \tau \leq t}} (h_{m\tau} - s_{m\tau}) \qquad m \, \epsilon \, M$$
$$t \, \epsilon \, T$$

MARKET REQUIREMENTS

$$(4.28) \qquad x_{ct} + v_{ct} \geq d_{ct} \qquad\qquad c \, \epsilon \, CF$$
$$t \, \epsilon \, T$$

EXPORT BOUNDS

$$(4.29) \qquad e_{ct} \leq \bar{e}_{ct} \qquad\qquad c \, \epsilon \, (CI \cup CF)$$
$$t \, \epsilon \, T$$

INVESTMENT CONSTRAINTS

$$(4.30) \qquad h_{mt} \leq \bar{h}_{mt} \, y_{mt} \qquad\qquad m \, \epsilon \, M$$
$$t \, \epsilon \, T$$

$$(4.31) \qquad y_{mt} = 0 \text{ or } 1 \qquad\qquad m \, \epsilon \, M$$
$$t \, \epsilon \, T$$

NONNEGATIVITY CONSTRAINTS

$$(4.32) \qquad
\begin{cases}
z_{pt} \geq 0 & p \, \epsilon \, P, & t \, \epsilon \, T \\
x_{ct} \geq 0 & c \, \epsilon \, CF, & t \, \epsilon \, T \\
e_{ct} \geq 0 & c \, \epsilon \, (CI \cup CF), & t \, \epsilon \, T \\
v_{ct} \geq 0 & c \, \epsilon \, (CF \cup CI \cup CR), & t \, \epsilon \, T \\
u_{ct} \geq 0 & c \, \epsilon \, CR, & t \, \epsilon \, T \\
h_{mt} \geq 0 & h \, \epsilon \, H, & t \, \epsilon \, T \\
y_{mt} \geq 0 & m \, \epsilon \, M, & t \, \epsilon \, T \\
w_{ct} \geq 0 & c \, \epsilon \, CI, & t \, \epsilon \, T
\end{cases}$$

The investment variables in this model, h_{mt}, reflect the fact that only scale and time-phasing are being considered (as well as the productive unit in which the investment is being made). If the productive unit subscript m is also dropped from the model, then it becomes one of pure time-phasing and scale.

The LEGO Set

Each individual application of a project selection model requires the introduction of a variety of constraints that are specific to the particular problem. A number of such constraints will be discussed here with the understanding that the analyst may want to select one or more of them to add to or use as a replacement for the model above in the process of constructing an appropriate model. Clearly, it is not possible to be exhaustive, and this section intends only to give the reader a feel for how the model can be built up to fit a particular case by giving two examples.

Substitution among final products

In the model above, market requirements have been stated so that they exclude any substitution among final commodities in meeting consumer requirements. The reverse of this polar case may be found in the fertilizer industry in which a number of different fertilizers can supply the required nutrients; for example, either or both ammonium sulfate and ammonium nitrate can be used to provide nitrogen nutrients. In such a case, the market requirements constraint (4.5) can be rewritten as:

$$(4.33) \qquad \sum_{c \in CF} \alpha_{cc'} \left[\sum_{i \in I} x_{cijt} + v_{cjt} \right] \geq d_{c'jt}, \qquad \begin{array}{l} c' \in CQ \\ j \in J \\ t \in T \end{array}$$

where shipments of domestic output (x_{cijt}) and imports (v_{cjt}) are expressed in terms of final products, market requirements ($d_{c'jt}$) are expressed in terms of nutrients contained in final products, $\alpha_{cc'}$ is the conversion factor expressing attribute (nutrient) c' of product c, and CQ is the set of final product requirements, namely, nitrogen and phosphorous in the fertilizer example.

Export constraints

Another set of constraints that can be used are varieties of export constraints. Two such constraints are:

$$(4.34) \qquad \sum_{i \in I} \sum_{l \in L} e_{cilt} \leq \bar{e}_{ct} \qquad \begin{array}{l} c \in (CF \cup CI) \\ t \in T \end{array}$$

and

$$(4.35) \qquad \sum_{c \epsilon CF} \sum_{i \epsilon I} e_{cilt} \leq \bar{e}_{lt}, \qquad \begin{matrix} l \epsilon L \\ t \epsilon T \end{matrix}$$

where

$\bar{e}_{ct}$ = an upper bound on the amount of commodity c that can be exported in year t without unduly forcing down the price,

$\bar{e}_{lt}$ = an upper bound on the amount of exports of all commodity types that export market l could reasonably be expected to purchase in year t.

These and other export bounds in the model may be needed to take account of the fact that the linear model imperfectly reflects market conditions. Another alternative formulation is to include piecewise linear demand functions for exports.

Care should be taken in specifying the export constraints because they may be extremely important in determining the character of the investment program. If exports are efficient, at a given price, the export bounds determine up to what point this outlet can be exploited and therefore affect the size of plants. At the same time, if they are specified at an unrealistically high level, they may result in the construction of the technically maximal plant size. For this reason, it may be preferable to specify a downward sloping demand curve for exports rather than the perfectly elastic one used now. To be handled in the framework of a linear program, the downward sloping demand curve would need to be approximated by a series of linear segments.

5

Data

THE DATA REQUIREMENTS of project selection models are much like those of any other microeconomic problem: demand, supply, and prices. This data base may be large or small, depending on the specification of the model and the degree of disaggregation. This chapter begins with a discussion of the data requirements of the complete model and then indicates how these data requirements are reduced as the specification of the model is simplified. In a parallel vein, the chapter points out how the scope of the project selection study must alter as the model specification and data requirements simplify and decrease.

Set Specification

The first step in data acquisition is set specification: that is, determination of the degree of disaggregation of the problem and units on which data is to be collected. The sets to be specified are: plant sites, I; domestic markets, J; export markets, L; productive units, M; processes, P; time periods, T; and commodities, C.

Plant sites

The determination of the set of plant sites, I, is ordinarily rather easy. Most industries require specific inputs that are not ubiquitous and are available either from a limited number of sites within the country or through imports from abroad. Apart from the supply of raw materials, site selection will also depend on the availability of roads, the supply of water and power, and the possibilities for waste disposal. Finally, the selection of sites will be influenced by the dispersion of demand. The latter may lead to an increase in the number of possible plant sites, although the increase will often be small, because demand tends to be concentrated around a limited number of marketing centers.

Fairly simple calculations may enable a reduction in the number of possible plant sites; in particular, it will sometimes be possible to determine beforehand whether the selection of a site should be based on the location of available inputs or on the location of demand. Often, feasibility studies that have investigated the desirability of establishing new plants or expanding existing plants are available; a number of possible sites can emerge from these studies. In addition, in some industries almost all of the expansion of capacity will ordinarily be made by increasing the capacity of productive units at existing plant sites, so the problem of specifying the set of plant sites is predetermined.

In a sectoral planning framework, however, as opposed to a project evaluation framework, it may be worthwhile to increase the set of plant sites beyond those sites that first come to mind. The reason for this is that efficiency considerations are frequently not the only considerations in project selection decisions. Political or environmental considerations may play a role. Also, a certain priority may be given to decentralized economic development, and the policymaker may be prepared to incur certain costs to achieve this objective. In such cases, the model can be used to indicate how much more it would cost the country if the plant were located in a less efficient but for other reasons more desirable spot.

Similarly, in a multicountry model it may be desirable to include plant sites in some countries that seem to be unlikely locations. Negotiations among countries participating in an integration scheme may result in certain industries being established in relatively inefficient locations in order that a politically acceptable mix of investments among countries can be obtained. Once again, the role of the economic model in such cases is not restricted to the selection of the optimal plant sites; it can provide a highly efficient method of calculating the cost of many alternative project sites.

Domestic markets

The selection of the set of marketing centers, *J*, depends primarily on the degree of disaggregation desired in the model. More marketing centers permit a more accurate calculation of the transport cost implications of project selection, which may be of particular importance if an inland location that competes with imports from abroad is considered.[1] If a substantial proportion of demand is located inland as well, the natural protection enjoyed by the inland plant compared with imports on account of transport cost savings may well open up investment possibilities that would have been ignored had the market been aggregated.

Export markets

In many cases, only a single export market area will be required, so that the set *L* will consist of a single element. The exceptions to this rule occur when export price discrimination is practiced or when export bounds for different markets (for example, of the type contained in the LEGO set) need to be incorporated.

Productive units

The productive units included in the set *M* should be the major units of the plant—in a steel mill they would include units such as the blast furnace, the steel shop, the continuous casters, and so forth. One rule to follow for disaggregation is to include an element in the set *M* for each major item in an investment program. For example, if the program could include either a direct reduction unit or a blast furnace, then separate elements should be included in the set *M* for each of these. Also, as indicated earlier, the set of productive units will frequently differ from plant to plant. As a rule, disaggregation among the productive units permits greater precision in the selection of a project or a program. On the other hand, it increases the complexity of the resulting model, particularly in the presence of econo-

---

1. One of the reviewers of a draft of this book pointed out that the assumption of proportional transport cost may be less likely to hold as the degree of market disaggregation increases.

mies of scale. If economies of scale are not present, greater disaggregation can be obtained without seriously increasing the computational cost of solving the model.

A difficulty that may arise in the specification of the set of productive units relates to the interdependent nature of many economic activities and to the impact this interdependence may have on the production cost structure of the relevant productive units. For this reason, it is often difficult to delineate the set of productive units that needs to be included in the model, and the analyst will then be required to use a fair amount of judgment about where to draw the line. To give an example, sulfuric acid is used in many activities outside the fertilizer industry. Clearly, an unmanageably large model would result if a detailed fertilizer model would have to be linked to similarly detailed models of all other sets of productive units that use sulfuric acid. In that case, the analyst must resort to making an estimate of the demand for sulfuric acid for uses outside the industry under study—and leave it at that. If the estimated uses outside the industry are very small, this difficulty is of small importance.

Processes

The set of processes, P, will depend primarily on the productive unit; frequently, however, there will be several alternative processes for each productive unit. For example, alternative processes for making pig iron with different mixes of pellets, sinter, and lump ore may be included in a steel industry model. The current economics of the industry may indicate that the pellet process dominates the sinter process. If it seems possible that a change in the relative prices of these inputs could alter the situation, however, then it would be desirable to include both processes in the set P.

Time periods

The selection of time periods in the set T turns on the question of model size. In general, it is desirable to have a longer horizon and more time periods. For many industrial planning models, it would be useful to have a model with a time horizon of twenty-five years, and annual time periods. Such a specification, however, will usually make the model much too large. A more common specification is a horizon of fifteen years, with three time periods of five years each or, perhaps, five time periods of three years each. Because it is implicitly assumed in the model that production levels are the same for all time intervals (years) within a time period, the quality of this approximation will not be good in a rapidly growing industry. In such cases, there is no alternative to a large number of short time periods, and savings in terms of model size may have to be found in the specification of other sets in the model.

Commodities

The set of commodities, C, should be chosen to include only the major final, intermediate, and raw material products, as well as the labor inputs. The ordinary specification is from five to ten final products and roughly the same number of intermediate products. If the set of constraints in (4.3) of chapter 4 (the balance equations for domestic and imported raw materials and for labor) are treated as equalities and are substituted out of the model, greater disaggregation of these inputs is desirable. In such a case, adding to the degree of disaggregation does not increase the number of variables or constraints. Because of the possibility of substituting out constraints (4.2) and (4.3), it will ordinarily be worthwhile to disaggregate the set of raw materials, miscellaneous inputs, and labor inputs CR into the domestic, imported, and domestic-imported subsets CRD, CRI, and $CRDI$. Then, the CRD and CRI constraints are substituted out, leaving only the $CRDI$ constraints in the programming problem.

Demand

In order to implement a project selection model, data are required for final products for both domestic and foreign demand.

Estimation and projection

An estimate of present and future demand is required for each final product in the model (d_{cjt}—$c\epsilon C$, $j\epsilon J$, $t\epsilon T$). In most cases, a combination of foreign trade and production statistics may provide a convenient source for the estimate of current demand. Sometimes, however, import statistics are not sufficiently disaggregated, in which case the task of demand estimation is more difficult. Several possibilities usually exist. One fairly laborious method of obtaining better estimates of current demand is to inspect the import licenses for a recent year or to survey importers as well as domestic producers and wholesale distributors. A more convenient alternative may present itself if a recent feasibility study was produced for the product in question. At worst, available estimates of demand for other countries at similar income levels may have to be used, corrected for differences in size of population.

Based on estimates of current demand, a projection of demand for the relevant planning period needs to be made. This is usually the most difficult part of a project planning study, for a variety of reasons. First, all projections about the future are hazardous, and economic projections are no exception to this general rule. Second, and more specific to project planning problems, a projection of demand for a specific product cannot be carried out independently of a forecast of the supply price. The latter will not be known until the investment program is selected and implemented. Given these problems, the most that can usually be hoped for is a plausible range of levels of future demand that make sense a priori given past growth rates of demand, and in the light of whatever cross-country information is available. The sectoral planning methods described in this and subsequent volumes have the advantage that the sensitivity of an investment program to varying projections of demand can be determined rapidly.

A serious complication, affecting both the estimation of current demand and the projection of future demand, occurs if close substitutes exist for one or more of the final products in the model. In such cases, demand figures should be produced for the set of substitutable products, under some common denominator, and the model will determine on the basis of price differences which specific products will eventually meet the market requirements. This situation occurs, for example, in the fertilizer industry, in which several products may supply a specific plant nutrient. In that case, demand requirements may be expressed in terms of the relevant nutrient, and the model is used to determine the least-cost product mix. Another example is the energy industry, in which the final demand might be specified in British thermal units (BTU's) and a number of products can be substituted for one another in meeting this demand.

In addition to the projection of domestic demand for final products, an estimate of likely future exports is required (e_{clt} where $c \epsilon CF$, $l \epsilon L$, $t \epsilon T$). Here, not much can be said in general because the prospects for export sales depend on a number of product-specific and area-specific characteristics. If a country has no particularly favorable raw material position or skilled labor force, it is usually prudent to be fairly pessimistic about exports. On the other hand, if a good raw material position is combined with a tight world market for related intermediate or final products, it is necessary to allow for the possibility of substantial exports. In selecting the appropriate export bounds, it may be necessary to take into account that a relatively low supply price alone does not guarantee exports, and that quality, stability of supply, and, often, an extensive sales apparatus are conditions for a successful export program. This may be reflected in export bounds that are gradually increasing over time. As in the case of a domestic demand projection, the objective may frequently be to come up with plausible export targets, based on the judgment of the project or sector analyst, on whatever information can be gathered from past performance, and on achievements by other countries.

Geographic and product distribution

The disaggregation of the market permits a more accurate calculation of transport cost and, therefore, of the cost differentials associated with alternative locational patterns. Disaggregation, however, compounds the problems associated with estimation and projection of demand. Often, it is sufficient to obtain estimates of current demand in each marketing center and to apply the projected overall growth rate of demand to each one. It is preferable, however, to have more detailed information on the likely growth of demand in each marketing center; this may sometimes be the case for industries such as the fertilizer industry if detailed agricultural plans for various regions are available. The fertilizer industry also provides an example of the need for product specification. Demand for fertilizers may be projected in terms of major nutrients rather than of fertilizer material, and, if such projections are combined with fertilizer recommendations, the demand projection in nutrients can be converted into detailed demand projections for specific fertilizer products.

Supply

Information is required on the current supply situation regarding the products as well as the factors of production specified in the model.

Capacity

Usually, it is fairly easy to obtain accurate data on existing capacity for the production of the commodities in the model (k_{mi} where $m \epsilon M$, $i \epsilon I$). It may be more difficult to obtain firm estimates on when existing capacity is likely to be scrapped (s_{mit} where $m \epsilon M$, $i \epsilon I$, $t \epsilon T$), and, unless announced plans for the elimination of capacity are known, it is probably better to assume that capacity available at the beginning of the planning period will continue to be in existence throughout the planning period.[2] Estimates of capacity are required for relevant raw material supplies as well; the difficulty here depends essentially on whether or not a raw material survey has been carried out. A distinction should be drawn between depletable and renewable resources in this context.[3] In the case of depletable resources, a further distinction should be drawn between proven and potential reserves, where the latter may be suspected only. Since the estimate of potential reserves is by definition crude, the best procedure may be at first to consider proven reserves only and to determine whether raw material supply poses a serious constraint on the investment program; if this occurs, further investigation of potential reserves may be worthwhile. For renewable resources, chiefly from forestry and agriculture, the raw material supply situation is itself subject to project or program planning; unless supply can be assumed to be adequate regardless of the dimension of the investment program under study, the raw-material–producing activity should be included in the investment planning model, so that the availability of raw materials is determined as a function of the investment program in the raw-material–using activities.

The project selection model requires the specification of upper bounds on the capacity that can be constructed for each productive unit (h_{mit} where $m \epsilon M$, $i \epsilon I$, $t \epsilon T$). Ordinarily, this bound should reflect

---

2. Whether or not existing capacity is utilized is determined by the model. Also, retirement decisions should in many cases not be treated as fixed but should be solved for within the model. In this case the s variables become like the y variables and should be treated in a similar fashion.

3. The model in chapter 4 does not include specific constraints for depletable resources. These could be added to the model by specifying that the stock of resources in a given time period equals the stock available in the previous period plus new discoveries minus use.

the technical limit on the size of productive units, and a good approximation for this bound may be the largest productive unit currently in operation. If it is unlikely that the project selection model will come up with capacity expansion plans that are close to such maximum sizes, because of market limitations; any arbitrary large number may be chosen to represent the upper bound.

Production

Relatively little information is needed on actual production levels in the set of productive units under study. In fact, production levels for final products need to be estimated only when domestic production figures are used to determine current levels of demand (in combination with import and export statistics). Requirements for new capacity in all productive units are generated by the model, comparing capacities installed at the beginning of the planning period with total requirements in the course of the planning period. The supply of labor and capital may have to be specified separately depending on the activity or set of activities under study and depending on the country. With respect to labor, the supply of certain kinds of skills may sometimes be limited, in which case the model needs to specify the constraints. For capital, it may be useful to draw a distinction between foreign and domestic capital and to specify relevant budget constraints for each. The determination of appropriate bounds for production factors is often difficult; initially, it may be sensible to assume that the availability of production factors is unlimited and to consider the feasibility of implementing any investment program independently of the model. If it appears that the requirements for one or more production factors are likely to be larger than supply, the model can be rerun, this time incorporating constraints reflecting this limitation.

Input-output relations

Information is required on the input-output coefficients (a_{cpi} where $c\epsilon C$, $p\epsilon P$, $i\epsilon I$) that link the commodities in the model. These are expressed in physical terms, usually taking the form of a quantity of a specific input required to produce a standard quantity (a ton, a bushel) of a specific output. Most of these input-output coefficients are of a standard type, and they can be obtained from a variety of technical publications, feasibility studies, and so forth. On occasion, problems may be encountered. First, inputs (either raw materials or intermediates) may be of varying quality, which will usually have an effect on the magnitude of the input-output coefficient. For example, the quantity of phosphate rock required to produce a ton of single superphosphate varies with the grade of the rock. Second, different productive processes for the production of the same commodity are not necessarily equally efficient in the use of various inputs. If different productive units employ equipment of varying vintage, it may be necessary to specify different input-output coefficients for each.

Furthermore, information is required on the capacity utilization coefficient (b_{mpi} where $m \epsilon M$, $p \epsilon P$, $i \epsilon I$), which denotes the number of units of capacity used on machine or productive unit m per unit of output of process P at plant i. This is not a serious problem, if there is a one-to-one relationship between capacity and output. For example, the production of 1 ton of nitric acid requires 1 ton of capacity in a nitric acid plant. In other cases, when machines or productive units are of a multipurpose nature, the relationship between capacity and output has to be expressed in different terms—for example, the number of hours of machine time required per unit of output. Whenever this is appropriate, data that express such product-specific equipment input requirements are required.

Prices and Costs

The set of price data needed for the implementation of a project selection model plays an important role in the selection process. Data on prices must be collected on current inputs, capital inputs, product prices, and transport cost. Each of these categories is discussed separately.

Current inputs

Price information is required on all current inputs (p^d_{cit} where $c \epsilon CRD \cup CRDI$, $i \epsilon I$, $t \epsilon T$; and p^v_{cit} where $c \epsilon CI \cup CRI \cup CRDI$, $i \epsilon I$, $t \epsilon T$) of which production is not considered explicitly in the set of specified productive units. This means that such information is needed on all relevant raw materials (whether of domestic or foreign origin), on imported intermediates, on labor inputs by relevant skill category, and on all miscellaneous inputs (domestic and foreign). The miscellaneous category of inputs contains all inputs into the productive process for which the availability is not in doubt and for which prices can be assumed as independent of the investment program.

Domestic raw materials should be priced at their opportunity cost; the simplest way to approximate opportunity cost is to equate it to the obtainable export price at the mine. What is needed is the projected export price at the mine. This price may be assumed to move parallel to the projected c.i.f. (including cost, insurance, and freight) import price for the same raw material, which also needs to be estimated. Possible sources for the import price include the World Bank's commodity price forecasts.

In the case of intermediate inputs, which may be produced in the set of productive units specified in the model, only the import price needs to be projected. The supply price of such intermediate inputs produced domestically will be generated by the model.

The detail about what information is required regarding projected wage cost depends to a large extent on the sector under study. In the heavy industry sector, direct labor inputs are often relatively small, and in some cases it is justified to include labor cost among the miscellaneous inputs. In agriculture, on the other hand, labor supply and wage cost are often of the essence in the design of a production program, and, in that case, very detailed price information will be necessary. If labor inputs are small, it may often not be worthwhile to carry out an elaborate analysis on the appropriate shadow price for labor. In all other cases, the determination of such prices is desirable, but, because the problems involved vary from sector to sector, it is preferable to discuss possible procedures in sector-specific volumes. Here, we shall confine ourselves to stating once more that the selection models proposed in this volume lend themselves well to an efficient assessment of the impact of a range of shadow prices for labor. In many cases it may be advisable, before embarking upon the difficult task of estimating the correct shadow price of labor, to determine whether variations in the wage rate structure have a noticeable impact on the selection and design of an investment project or program.

Finally, the prices associated with miscellaneous inputs need to be estimated for the planning period. Since these are assumed to be available in sufficient quantities at prices that are not influenced by the investment program, their supply prices may not be too difficult to estimate. In addition, because these inputs will usually be of minor importance in the production process, estimation errors may not have much impact.

Capital inputs

For each productive unit and for each productive process within each unit, estimates are required for the capital costs to be incurred over the range of permissible activity levels (ω_{mit} and v_{mit} where $m \epsilon M$, $i \epsilon I$, $t \epsilon T$). For many activities, estimates of capital costs can be obtained in the form of investment cost functions from technical publications, trade journals, and feasibility studies. For industrial plants, many sources give such estimates in the form of "battery-limits" investment costs, which are the costs of plant and equipment in an equipment-producing country; this cost estimate excludes the transport cost of the equipment to the importing country, the cost of plant installation, the cost of country-specific contingencies, and the cost of off-site facilities. The markup for the latter cost categories varies from country to country, depending on the country's level of development and the distance from equipment suppliers. It is likely that in any given country the markup is fairly uniform across sectors, and the markup actually recorded for investments in the same sector in the country or in comparable neighboring countries may give a reasonable approximation of the appropriate adjustment. A more systematic effort to collect data on investment cost—including information on capacity constructed, year(s) in which construction takes place, gestation period, and location—could facilitate the task of estimating investment cost considerably. Another factor to take into account in estimating capital costs is the impact of inflation on equipment costs. Most trade journals produce price indexes for equipment, and the sector-specific volumes will give references for this purpose.

Many empirical studies have been carried out on the form of the investment function in various sectors, and several references to such studies on activities with economies of scale were given in chapter 1. It appears that in many cases the investment cost function can be expressed as an exponential function, with fairly constant elasticity over a wide range of capacities. Often, for industrial activities, the elasticity of plant investments in relation to capacity is between 0.6 and 0.8.

In addition to the estimation of investment costs, information is needed on the lifetime of plant and equipment (ζ_m where $m \epsilon M$), as well as on the appropriate price of capital. A distinction should be drawn between economic and technical lifetime: the latter indicates the technical durability of the investment; the former, the period during which the investment can be expected to be economically efficient. Sometimes, the distinction is of little significance, for example, in the case of a dam, which has a long technical and economic lifetime, or in the case of motor vehicles, which have short economic and technical lifetimes. The most serious problems occur in the case of industrial plant and equipment. Technical lifetimes may be long, particularly if proper maintenance takes place. In the past, economic lifetimes have varied widely, from a range of five to ten years in some petrochemical activities, to a range of twenty to thirty years in cement production. Strictly speaking, the economic lifetime of investments should be determined by the project selection model, by incorporating technology forecasts in the investment cost data and letting the model determine the optimal timing for a switch from one technology to another. Such technology forecasts are difficult to make, however, Moreover, the use of the capital recovery factor requires that the economic lifetime of the new investments is postulated. For pragmatic reasons, therefore, it is suggested that the plant and equipment lifetimes are estimated on the basis of past experience, combined with the expectations of sector specialists regarding the likely rate at which significant technological innovations may take place. Guidelines for estimating plant and equipment lifetimes in specific sectors will be given in subsequent volumes.

With respect to the price of capital, an argument similar to that used for labor costs applies. Within the partial-equilibrium framework in which project and program selection is carried out, it is not possible to come up with the correct shadow price for capital. In fact, the project selection approach proposed in this volume enables a slightly different approach to the problem of capital costs. Often, project financiers or planners have a cutoff rate of return on capital, below which the establishment of a project is not normally considered. If this cutoff rate of return is known a priori, it can be taken as the interest rate in the model, so that the project selection exercise results in the reporting of only those projects and programs that have an internal rate of return equal to the cutoff rate or better; if none of the projects meets this standard, the model will recommend a policy of all imports. In this case, the formulation of the model changes slightly, because now the rate of interest and the rate of discount in the model are no longer identical; ρ in the capital recovery factor should then be replaced by $\hat{\rho}$ where the latter denotes the cutoff interest rate. If the cutoff rate is not known, several can be postulated and it can be investigated whether investment projects or programs are feasible at various prices of capital, and what impact variations in this price have on the selection of the program.[4]

Product prices

In addition to the current input prices that need to be estimated and projected, c.i.f. import and f.o.b. (free on board) export prices for final and intermediate products (p^v_{cjt} where $c \epsilon CF \cup CI$, $j \epsilon J$, $t \epsilon T$; p^v_{cit} where $c \epsilon CF \cup CI$, $i \epsilon I$, $t \epsilon T$; p^c_{cilt} where $c \epsilon CF$, $i \epsilon I$, $l \epsilon L$, $t \epsilon T$) speci-fied in the model need to be projected. Long-term projections of im-port and export prices are extremely difficult to make, and the analyst has to allow for a wide margin of error. This is an unfortunate com-plication that every economic planner has to live with, and project analysts are by no means exceptions to the rule. Once more, however, the user of a project selection model has the advantage that he can rapidly test out the implications of a range of import and export price projections on the investment project or program and he can recom-mend the one that is based on the projection that in his judgment is the most likely to prevail. As a rule, therefore, the practitioner is ad-vised to select at least three pairs of import and export price levels (the latter well below the former—by 30 to 40 percent), labeling one pair unlikely high, one unlikely low, and one with prices in be-tween these two extremes. If it is distinctly possible that imports will not be available, an alternative is to place the import price at infinity.

Another set of product prices that needs to be projected relates to by-product sales (p^d_{cit} where $c \epsilon CI$, $i \epsilon I$, $t \epsilon T$). If such products are im-ported from abroad at the beginning of the planning period, the appropriate price attainable for such products is the projected import price. If they are already available domestically from other sources, the recorded price should give a basis for the projection.

---

4. In times and places of high inflation, there may be a substantial difference between the real and the nominal rates of interest since the nominal rate is equal to the real rate plus the rate of inflation. Our tendency is to deflate all costs and prices and solve the model in real terms. In this case, the real rather than the nominal rate of interest should be used.

Transport cost

The transport cost information (μ_{cijt} where $c \epsilon CF$, $i \epsilon I$, $j \epsilon J$, $t \epsilon T$; μ_{cjt} where $c \epsilon CF$, $j \epsilon J$, $t \epsilon T$; μ_{cit} where $c \epsilon CI \cup CRD \cup CRDI$, $i \epsilon I$, $t \epsilon T$; μ_{cilt} where $c \epsilon CF \cup CI$, $i \epsilon I$, $l \epsilon L$, $t \epsilon T$; and $\mu_{cii't}$ where $c \epsilon CI$, $i \epsilon I$, $i' \epsilon I$, $t \epsilon T$) usually requires substantial research. Often, alternative transport modes—including road, rail, water, and, sometimes, air transport—are available or feasible. If they are available, transport costs between plant and raw material sites, marketing centers, and import and export points can usually be obtained from published tariff handbooks. If they are not available, geographic distances need to be determined, and they need to be combined with approximations to what appears a reasonable transport cost function for the area, based either on incomplete country- and product-specific information or, at worst, on cross-country information. A serious problem can occur if plant sites and marketing centers that have no good transport links need to be included in the model. In such cases, it may be necessary to specify the model with and without the construction of a road, railroad, and, in the case of substantial projected exports, port facilities, as a component of the investment program. The proportion of these costs charged to the investment program would be dependent upon which other activities are estimated to benefit from the transport investment.

Other Data for the Complete Model

In addition to the data requirements specified above, a rate of discount should be postulated, as well as the appropriate rate of foreign exchange. The discount rate, ρ, which does not have to be equal to the interest charges on capital even though it often is taken to be equal, plays an important role in the selection and design of an investment project or program, and in particular influences the optimal timing of investments. At the same time, it is difficult to make a strong case for a particular value of the discount rate. Usually, the discount rate is placed at a value ranging from 10 to 15 percent. It is strongly recommended to allow for parametric variation in the discount rate to determine the impact of different discount rates on the optimal program design.

The choice of the appropriate rate of foreign exchange is a difficult problem, plaguing every phase of project planning.[5] For purposes of project selection, the following procedure is recommended. The official exchange rate is used for converting all imports and exports into domestic currency, and the project selection exercise is carried out on the basis of these values. For each feasible investment program, the domestic resource cost of saving one unit of foreign exchange is calculated next, and subsequent volumes will give detailed guidelines on how this calculation is most efficiently performed. The domestic resource cost of saving foreign exchange should then be compared with the official exchange rate. This comparison will provide the project analyst with a basis for judging whether or not the proposed investment program is attractive—this judgment is usually based on a hunch about the range in which the correct shadow price for foreign exchange should lie rather than on a precise computation of such an exchange rate. As in the case of the shadow prices for labor and capital, therefore, the project selection model permits a more flexible approach than is usually possible in the project evaluation phase.

Data Requirements for Variants of the Complete Model

The previously described data requirements apply when the complete project selection model needs to be solved numerically. Obviously, if less than the complete model appears appropriate, the data requirements will be correspondingly less. Conversely, if not all data can be obtained, the project analyst will have to be content with a project selection model that is restricted in scope or precision. In this section, a few of the possibilities are discussed, although no attempt is made to be exhaustive.

Data requirements for modified project selection models

Possible modifications to the project selection model may be related to the dynamic nature of the model or to the locational choice.

---

5. The foreign exchange rate is not shown explicitly in the model, but it is implicit in import and export prices, and in investment cost.

Less important, the project analyst may not be interested in product-mix problems but may be content with the deletion of export activities, by-product sales, and the like. Also, the project analyst may not attach much importance to options with respect to the selection of scale. For example, in certain cases of dam construction, the scale of the dam might be considered predetermined, and the model specification may be modified accordingly.[6] In the overwhelming number of cases, however, predetermined project scales are illegitimate, and extreme care should generally be exercised before this modification to the selection model is made.

If a static project selection model is all that is considered necessary, the data requirements for the model's numerical implementation are substantially reduced. The demand projection for final products, the establishment of bounds on exports and by-product sales, and the projection of import prices for raw materials, intermediates, and final products need to be made for a single year or period only. If the projection year is in the near future—which will often be the case for this type of planning problem—greater confidence can usually be placed on the projection. On the other hand, the static model can not consider the issue of optimal timing of capacity construction, and, in the presence of economies of scale, this may lead to smaller than optimal plant sizes. Because multiperiod projections are hazardous to make, however, the cost of building plants that are too large must be traded off against the cost of building plants that are too small.

If the siting of a project is not at issue—for example, only one location needs to be considered for a variety of reasons—the data requirements for the project selection model will be affected. They are most importantly affected if the predetermined site is identical or close to the only importing point, because in that case neither the domestic transport cost nor the regional specification of demand is required. On the other hand, if the predetermined location is substantially distant from the importing point, data requirements are affected only marginally, in the sense that it is only transport cost estimates for interplant shipments that are now no longer relevant. Only in very special cases, therefore, will a restricted locational choice result in lesser data requirements.

---

6. Factors such as the size of the reservoir and the length of canals would still be open to choice.

The effect of incomplete data on model specification

A major objection to the use of project selection models of the type discussed in this volume is that often they cannot be applied because of the lack of data. This criticism is made particularly with respect to their use in developing countries. Indeed, the number of data needed to implement the complete project selection model is substantial. Two issues should, however, be stressed here. First, the data requirements do not depend on the method of analysis; rather, they depend on which questions are addressed in the project planning exercise. Fewer data must result in a less accurate project selection study. Second, it is not necessary that a complete set of data be available to render the project selection model a useful tool of analysis. If no detailed year-by-year demand projection can be made, a static model is better than no model at all. Similarly, if no regional breakdown of demand can be estimated with any degree of accuracy, a spatially aggregated model is a second-best alternative. Moreover, as was indicated repeatedly during the discussion of the data requirements for the complete model, it is often impossible to come up with firm estimates or projections in any environment, and it is precisely under those circumstances that the project selection model provides a useful tool, because it permits the rapid assessment of the impact of a variety of values for certain variables.

In most cases, even with a limited amount of data, it should be possible to design a set of rough estimates for essentially unknown variables and parameters, placing these at values that area and sector specialists consider unlikely high and unlikely low. Experimentation with values in between these two extremes may give the project analyst in many cases a good feel for what the optimal investment program would look like if better data were available.

In conclusion, it may be stated that the better the data, the better the project selection phase can be conducted. In the presence of incomplete data, the project selection model still possesses a number of features that can be exploited by the project analyst to aid him in the selection of an attractive project or program.

6

Uses of the Model

THE USE OF THE MODELS described in this volume can be characterized either by the area of their application or by their use. The areas
of application range from a single domestic company to the world as
a whole. Although the company models at first focused on internal
problems of plant management, the scope of application at the company level was gradually expanded. For example, at least one multinational company in the aluminum industry has used project selection
models for multicountry planning of capacities, optimal shipping patterns, and the like.[1] Increasingly, the advantages of the use of project
selection models are being recognized for national, regional, and worldwide project planning; although such models have rarely been used
for actual decisionmaking so far, a growing literature on the subject
is emerging.

Five uses of project selection models appear to be particularly
important: determination of efficient shipment patterns, project and

1. See Bruce T. Marcus and Arthur J. Ungar, "A Multi-period Two Stage
Model for Locating Alumina and Aluminum Reduction Capacity" (paper presented at the Institute for Management Science Meeting in Mexico City, August
1967), which discusses a model used by Kaiser Aluminum and Chemical
Corporation.

program selection, economic integration studies, export analysis, and industry regulation. These uses are discussed in this chapter.

Determination of Efficient Shipping Patterns

The project selection model can be used to study efficient shipment patterns if all the investment variables are set exogenously to the model. In this case, all capacity is assumed to be in place, and the only question posed is the determination of plant-to-market shipments of final products and plant-to-plant shipments of intermediate products. This exercise is ordinarily thought of as being done for a single-period model rather than for a multiperiod model. Then the problem is one of finding the shipment pattern for a set of plants that most efficiently uses the existing capacity. Since all the variables that enter into a plant decision are set exogenously, in this case the resulting computational problem is a linear program that can be solved very rapidly. A problem of this kind involving only a small number of plants or markets can be solved without the development of an elaborate model; when many productive units, plant sites, markets, and products are involved, however, substantial savings may be obtained through solution of a model.

An interesting application of the model for determining efficient shipment patterns is in the case of a multiperiod, spatially disaggregated model incorporating economies of scale; this application is related to the phenomenon that, under economies of scale, it is often efficient to construct a certain amount of overcapacity. If such a plant is constructed, the overcapacity during the initial years can be utilized for the production of output that is shipped to regions that would normally be outside the marketing area of the plant. Using excess capacity for this purpose is attractive as long as more than marginal cost of production plus transport cost can be covered, because then at least some contribution is made to the fixed cost as compared with none if excess capacity is left idle. As demand in the nearby regions grows over time, such distant shipments will contract in accordance with the objective of cost minimization. As a result of this policy, overcapacity may not show up in the actual production figures. The determination of efficient shipment patterns in such cases is, in the absence of a model, very difficult, whereas the solution of a model would automatically yield such patterns.[2]

Project and Program Selection

The application of the model for project and program selection corresponds to the full use of the model to study the size, location, and time-phasing of increments to capacity in a system of existing or potential plants. The investigation can be conducted in the context of a single company or sector, in a multisector setting, or on an economywide basis.

The use of the project selection model to determine the optimal investment program derives its main advantage from the fact that full account can be taken of the interdependencies among a specified set of activities. In the presence of economies of scale, these are primarily related to the circular relationship among demand and prices: whether a product is produced domestically or is imported from abroad depends on how domestic production cost compares with import cost. At the same time, domestic production cost depends on the scale at which production takes place and, therefore, on demand. This type of interdependence becomes particularly difficult to deal with if it affects intermediate products, especially intermediate products that can be used as inputs into a number of final products. In such cases, the project-by-project approach is clearly invalid, and a simultaneous investigation of the set of interdependent activities is called for.

A project selection model that focuses on this form of interdependence may come up with rather startling results. For example, a project may be included in the recommended investment program even though it appears to have a higher total cost than would have to be incurred if an equivalent quantity were imported. The explanation for this situation is that the comparison with import cost should not be made on the basis of the total cost of the project, but on the

2. If demand for the product is price elastic, less than full-cost pricing in the natural marketing region of the plant would increase demand, and this may be preferable to spatial price discrimination. As stated before, however, the present formulation of the project selection model does not incorporate price-elastic demand.

basis of total net cost associated with the project. The relevant test consists of determining what the impact on the total investment program would be if the project in question were deleted. Its presence in the recommended investment program implies that its net cost is lower than its total cost as a result of savings generated elsewhere in the program. This phenomenon will often occur because some intermediate product is produced on a larger scale, and thus at lower average cost, than would have been possible in the absence of the project.

If the data are available to formulate a spatially disaggregated model, another important aspect of project or program selection can be investigated—that is, the relative efficiency of domestic production as compared with imports, taking into account transport costs between plants and importing points, on the one hand, and between plants, importing points, and marketing centers, on the other hand. Particularly in the case of an inland location, this use of the model may be of importance in determining whether or not domestic production is to be preferred to imports on the basis of delivered cost.

A further characteristic of the complete project selection model is that it can be used to determine the most efficient timetable for expanding the capacity of a set of interdependent activities. Interdependence over time, in the presence of economies of scale, will often result in productive units being constructed at a scale that is somewhat ahead of demand. Moreover, taking into account simultaneously interdependencies among different productive units may often affect the timing of new capacity construction, once more because the project selection model employs the criterion of net cost rather than the narrower, project-specific criterion of total cost.

An important use of the full sectoral planning model is as a simulation device. For example, assume that a sectoral planning model has been solved for a particular set of activities in a given country. Independently, a feasibility study has been prepared that suggests the establishment of a project or set of projects of a design that is at variance with the one recommended on the basis of the project selection model. By fixing the relevant investment variables in the model so they are in accordance with those in the alternative proposal, the planning model can be used (a) to check the internal consistency of the alternative investment program and (b) to determine the relative ranking of this proposal to the investment programs identified with the use of the project selection model.

Alternatively, assume a situation in which a government is politically committed to locate a project or set of projects in a given sector in a specific region. The model can now be used to determine the least-cost investment program under this constraint, by simply restricting the choice in the model so that the desired minimum of investment occurs in the relevant region. The choices left open in that case could be, for example, scale and product mix.

These two examples should make clear that this type of application of the project selection model offers a wide range of possibilities. In fact, there is reason to believe that, in practice, the use of the model to calculate alternative solutions may outweigh all other potential uses in importance, reflecting the simple truth that choice in economics is restricted by many factors, not all of which are purely economic in nature.

Finally, the project selection model may be used as a framework for collecting and organizing data that are required for project analysis.[3] As later volumes in this series will show, a highly efficient form of data storage is provided if the data input format of the project selection model is followed. Even without further exploitation of the advantages that the model offers, this format permits easy access to a structured data set and, in the longer run, provides a rationale for the systematic collection of data that are often neglected or considered irrelevant to the project selection phase.

Economic Integration Studies

An important objective of economic integration arrangements among developing countries is to enable projects to be established at a more efficient scale than would have been possible on the basis of the domestic market of each of the individual countries alone. The use of the project selection model in that case is in many respects identical to the one described in the previous section, in the sense that the objective may be to determine the most efficient scale, timing, and location of a project or program for the integrated area. In practice, however, project selection in an integrated area is not identical

---

3. Since a variety of methods of project design and appraisal exist, it would be a mistake to tie the data collection to only a single method such as the mixed-integer programming models proposed in this book.

to project selection in a single country or company; the major complication is that political factors play a substantial role. The most important complicating factor is that countries are unlikely to agree to locating an integration project in a partner country, unless they are to obtain substantial advantages for themselves. These may take the form of lower prices than could be obtained from alternative supply sources. In practice, however, this has rarely turned out to be a sufficient incentive for an integration project agreement, and, increasingly, the so-called package approach is advocated.

The package approach involves the simultaneous allocation of a number of integration projects among the partner countries, so that each receives at least one regional project. The complications arising in the selection of a package of regional projects and the allocation of the projects among the participating countries are often enormous. Frequently, the political negotiations on the projects and their allocation will necessitate a redesign of the initial plan, and here the project selection model could play an important role. First, the condition that each country will receive at least one project can be explicitly modeled, and the least-cost allocation of projects subject to this constraint can be determined. Second, the model provides an opportunity to estimate the relative gains and losses associated with different investment programs for the area. This may be done by first calculating the net cost to be incurred by each country to meet specified requirements in isolation, and then by making a similar calculation for different coalitions of potential partner countries. Third, the project selection model can be used to accompany negotiations on the implementation of the agreement by providing a highly efficient tool to compute the quantitative implications for each country of various options for project allocation.

Export Analysis

The most cogent argument against economic integration studies of the kind discussed above is that political rivalries among nations preclude effective integration schemes. The world is littered with the wreckage of proposed common market agreements in Asia, Africa, and Latin America, and even the European Common Market is not without its problems. One alternative to economic integration among neighboring countries that have a similar objective of alleviating the restrictive effects of a small domestic market is to attempt to identify products that countries can successfully export to world markets.

To use the project selection model to its full advantage for this purpose, the following procedure could be adopted. First, the world is divided into a number of marketing regions, preferably consisting of a number of countries each, and market requirement estimates for a given set of related products are made, for a set of future years, much as was described in connection with the country application of the model. Estimates are also made of the cost of raw materials and the shipping cost between regions.

Second, a project selection model is solved to find the most efficient location for increments to capacity in the world at large, as well as the resulting shipping patterns. Having solved the model, a variety of new constraints on the problem can be introduced in an attempt to make the results more realistic. For example, constraints can be imposed on plant size to reflect managerial problems that may arise. Constraints also can be added to reflect that importing countries may desire a variety of sources for a given product, so as not to be dependent on one source of supply. A large number of other modifications to the original model can be made, depending on the specifics of the situation.

Various possible uses of this application of the model should be noted. First, the least-cost capacity expansion program and shipping pattern for the world provides a minimum estimate of the capital resources that are needed to meet the world's total requirement for the product(s) in question. Any deviation from the optimal program will necessarily result in higher capital or production costs, as well as higher transport cost.

Second, the model provides a tool for tracing the implications of a relatively "bad" project. To make this clear, assume that an independent agency has prepared a feasibility study recommending the establishment of a project in a given country, and that this project meets the economic and financial test that a project financier applies to determine whether the project qualifies for financing. Assume further that this project is not part of the optimal investment program resulting from the application of the global project selection model. Barring differences in the values of the relevant variables and parameters, the relatively inefficient project must have detrimental effects on other countries. The model can now be used to trace which countries are likely to suffer from a bad project, and judgments can then be made on the desirability of implementing the project, depending on whether the countries that are negatively affected are relatively well off. In other words, the application of the project selection model on a worldwide scale enables a quantification of the effects of a specific project on a third country. Such effects may occur even if the project is not export oriented in the sense that, even if it is purely import-substituting, it eliminates a market for a potential exporter.

Regulation

A final category of applications of the project selection model is in the area of regulation. Price regulation would seem to be an obvious possibility. This application is far from straightforward, however, because the optimal shipping pattern recommended by the model is based on marginal cost of production of each product (plus transport cost, if applicable), and not on total costs. Although the investment cost is taken into account in determining whether an investment program implies lower net total costs than imports, the investment charges remain unallocated by market. To use the model for purposes of price regulation, therefore, decisions must be made regarding the allocation of the fixed costs among users.

It may be a stated government objective to make certain products available to users at a price that is identical across the country, so as not to place remote regions at a disadvantage. The spatially disaggregated project selection model can be used to determine the nationwide price and the transfer payments that are required among plants in different locations and, ultimately, among users. The procedure to be followed is, first, to solve the model without the uniform-price restriction. For each marketing center, for each time period, and for each product in the model, the marginal delivered cost is obtained from the model's solution. Next, the total of the cost components that are not contained in the marginal delivered cost (investment charges and the capacity-related recurrent cost) is determined for each period, and it is allocated to each marketing center so that uniform supply prices result for each time period. The simplest way of doing this is to compute the sum total of quantity times delivered price as given by the model, for all domestic marketing centers taken together, and add to this sum the amount of investment charges and capacity-related recurrent cost (assuming no complications arising out of possible exports). Given the total quantity of output delivered, the uniform delivered price can now be calculated.

The model can also be used to determine a fair compensation in case of nationalization. In fact, the procedure to be followed for this application is quite simple. First, the industry to be nationalized, together with all appropriate interdependent activities, is represented by a model, and the model is solved, estimating the total net cost to be incurred to meet market requirements for the set of interdependent activities, for a period that is equal to the estimated lifetime of the industry to be nationalized. Next, the same model is solved, for the same timespan, but assuming that the industry to be nationalized does not exist. The difference between the total net cost associated with the first version of the model and that associated with the second version (both discounted to the present) should give the net value to the economy of the industry under discussion.

Concluding Remarks

The applications of the project selection model described in the preceding sections are intended to give a flavor of the uses to which such a model can be put. The description is by no means exhaustive, and in particular circumstances, for particular sets of activities, additional uses can be identified. One point, however, should be clear: the objective of a project selection model is not limited to the determination of the optimal investment project or program. Rather, the model should be seen as an efficient tool of project analysis, designed to guide the project analyst in choosing from among a large number of alternatives. Because the model is a simplified representation of reality, both its design and the interpretation of its results require the area-specific and sector-specific expertise of the project analyst to exploit fully its advantages.

7

Limitations of the Model

THE PROJECT SELECTION MODEL, as it is presented in this volume, has some important limitations that should be explicitly stated. Many of the limitations are specific to the formulation of the model as chosen here. A number of limitations, however, are of a more serious nature—that is, those which represent shortcomings in the state of the art. These are primarily associated with computer technology, and consequently they can be overcome only when further progress is achieved in the size of problems that can be handled by computers and in the efficiency of computational procedures required to obtain numerical solutions to such problems.[1]

Limitations in both areas will be discussed in this chapter, and, to the extent that it is possible, suggestions will be made about how particular shortcomings can be partly or wholly overcome. This format may give the chapter a somewhat apologetic character, although that is not our intention. With all its limitations, the project selection model in its current formulation represents a substantial improvement over more conventional methods of project identification and, if intelligent use is made of it, permits improved project planning. Moreover, rapid advances in computer technology not only will permit the application of project selection models at continually decreasing

---

1. The nature of the computational problem varies with the method of analysis chosen; for example, mixed-integer programming and dynamic programming may lead to different degrees of combinatorial problems.

cost, but also will enable the construction and application of increasingly more complex models, incorporating improved representation of the real world.

Methodological progress in this field stems largely from the experience gained from practical applications. Impetus will be given to this interactive process only if remaining shortcomings of the model are clearly identified at each stage. This not only provides an agenda for further research, but also aids the project analyst in determining the applicability of the methodology in specific situations and in interpreting the results of each application. This chapter is written in that spirit.

The Objective Function and Fixed Demands

One of the most important problems to be addressed in deciding upon the appropriate formulation of the project selection model is the choice of objective function; a related problem is the treatment of demand. The cost minimization formulation used in the models previously described has the virtue of being simple and of embodying the reasonable desire to produce a given quantity of goods with the minimum use of resources. Its limitation is that it assumes fixed demands rather than demand that is responsive to price.[2]

This limitation may not be too serious under some circumstances. First, the project selection model may cover products for which demand, over some range, is indeed insensitive to price. Second, the demand projection may have been carried out on the basis of supply prices that are fairly close to those which come out of the model. In the large majority of cases, however, the assumption of perfectly price-inelastic demand may be unrealistic.

Whenever the demand for final products is price elastic, the model results may be inconsistent, in the sense that market requirements may have been estimated on the basis of prices that differ from those implied by the solution to the model. If this is the case, one possible procedure is to solve the model repeatedly until the requirements implied by the two sets of prices are more or less similar. In the case

2. This limitation is by no means specific to the project selection model. By necessity, more conventional project selection methods also start off from some projection of demand for final products, before knowing the domestic supply price.

of many final products, however, this procedure may be cumbersome and costly.

An alternative approach to the incorporation of variable demand into the model is the consumers' and producers' surplus method outlined by T. Takayama and G. G. Judge and applied by J. H. Duloy and R. D. Norton to linear programming models.[3] The basic idea of this method, as originally developed by P. A. Samuelson, is that the competitive solution to a market problem can be obtained by solving an optimization problem in which consumers' and producers' surplus is maximized.[4] This result holds in the case that production is characterized by decreasing returns to scale. In the case of increasing returns to scale, the profit-maximizing output level for the individual firm is not the same as the output level that maximizes welfare. For this reason, both the problem of consumers' and producers' surplus and a problem that seeks the maximization of profit are described here.

First, consider the consumer-producer surplus maximization problem.[5] Let:

(7.1)
$$p_d = f(v),$$

and

(7.2)
$$p_s = s(x),$$

where

p_d = demand price,
p_s = supply price,
f = demand function,
s = supply function,
v = amount demanded, and
x = amount supplied.

The functions are plotted in figure 5.

3. See T. Takayama and G. G. Judge, *Spatial and Temporal Price and Allocation Models* (Amsterdam: North Holland Publishing Co., 1971); and John H. Duloy and Roger D. Norton, "Prices and Incomes in Linear Programming Models," *American Journal of Agricultural Economics*, vol. 57 (November 1975), pp. 591–600.

4. See P. A. Samuelson, "Spatial Price Equilibrium and Linear Programming," *American Economic Review*, vol. XLII (June 1952), pp. 283–303.

5. See Takayama and Judge, *Spatial and Temporal Price and Allocation Models*, chapter 6.

Figure 5. The Consumers' and Producers' Surplus

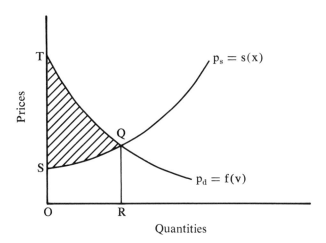

The consumers' and producers' surplus is the shaded area *SQT* in figure 5; it is equal to the area under the demand curve *ORQT* minus the area under the supply curve *ORQS*. If the consumers' and producers' surplus is defined as *W*, then:

$$(7.3) \qquad W = \int_0^v p_d d\eta - \int_0^x p_s d\xi,$$

where

    η = integration variable for v and
    ξ = integration variable for x.

The first term on the right-hand side of (7.3) is equal to the area under the demand curve, whereas the second term is equal to the area under the supply curve. If one views the area under the demand curve as the total satisfaction obtained from a commodity, and the area under the supply curve as the cost to society of obtaining that product, then *W* can be seen as a measure of the net benefit.

As an illustration of the use of this approach, consider a problem with a single commodity and with a linear demand function. Also, the area under the supply curve can be replaced with an unspecified cost function since the cost function in industrial planning models is not an explicit function, but is implicit in the technology specification, the prices of inputs, and so forth. Let us define:

$$(7.4) \qquad h(v) \equiv \int_0^v p_d \, d\eta \, .$$

Then,

$$(7.5) \qquad W = h(v) - c(x),$$

where

$h(v)$ = area under the demand curve,

$c(x)$ = cost of production and shipping.

If the linear demand function is defined as:

$$(7.6) \qquad p_d = a + bv, \qquad\qquad a > 0, b < 0$$

$h(v)$ can be rewritten as follows:

$$(7.7) \qquad h(v) = \int_0^v p_d \, d\eta = \int_0^v (a + b\eta) \, d\eta \, .$$

Carrying out the integration in (7.7) yields:

$$(7.8) \qquad h(v) \, [a\eta + \tfrac{1}{2} b\eta^2]^v = av + \tfrac{1}{2} bv^2,$$

and substitution of (7.8) into (7.5) yields:

$$(7.9) \qquad W = av + \tfrac{1}{2} bv^2 - c(x).$$

Since the project selection model is specified as a linear program, the cost function $c(x)$ will be piecewise linear, but the area under the demand curve is shown in (7.9) to be quadratic. Therefore, it is necessary to approximate the quadratic function $h(v)$ with a piecewise linear approximation. The function $h(v)$ and its approximation $\hat{h}(v)$ are shown in figure 6.

The approximating function $\hat{h}(v)$ is defined as[6]:

$$(7.10) \qquad \hat{h}(v) = \sum_k \delta_k \gamma_k \, ,$$

---

6. Ibid.

Figure 6. A Piecewise Linear Approximation to the Area
under the Demand Curve

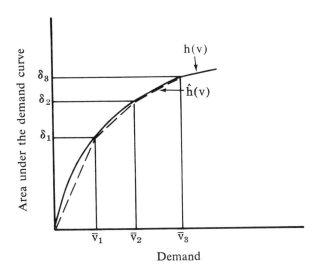

where

(7.11) $$\delta_k = h(\bar{v}_k),$$

and the points $\bar{v}_k$ are fixed grid points. Furthermore, it is required
that:

(7.12) $$\sum_k \gamma_k = 1,$$

and that:

(7.13) $$\gamma_k > 0 \text{ for all } k.$$

The approximation in Figure 7.2 is made by first choosing the grid
points $\bar{v}_k$ close enough together to provide a satisfactory approximation. These points, together with the true function $h(v)$, are used in
(7.11) to obtain the points δ_k. The variables γ_k then provide a convex
combination of the δ_k's, that is, they enable one to interpolate between
the δ_k's and thereby to approximate the true function $h(v)$ with the
dashed-line approximating function $\hat{h}(v)$.

Furthermore, the amount demanded is also a convex combination,
but it is a combination of the grid points v_k rather than of the δ_k's;

that is:

(7.14) $$v = \sum_k \bar{v}_k \, \gamma_k \, .$$

With this approximation, it can be shown how one can convert a simple cost-minimizing, fixed-demand model into a maximizing model with variable demand. Consider the simplest model discussed in chapter 3, that is:

(7.15) $$\min \xi = \sum_{i \in I} \sum_{j \in J} \mu_{ij} \, x_{ij} \, ,$$

subject to:

(7.16) $$\sum_{j \in J} x_{ij} \le k_i \, , \qquad\qquad i \in I$$

(7.17) $$\sum_{i \in I} x_{ij} \ge d_j \, , \qquad\qquad j \in J$$

(7.18) $$x_{ij} \ge 0, \qquad\qquad \begin{matrix} i \in I \\ j \in J \end{matrix}$$

where

x = shipments from plant i to market j,
μ = unit transportation costs,
k_i = production capacity at plant i, and
d_j = market requirements at market j.

This model can be rewritten as:

(7.19) $$\max \xi = \sum_j \sum_k \delta_{kj} \, \gamma_{kj} - \sum_i \sum_j \mu_{ij} \, x_{ij},$$

with

(7.20) $$\delta_{kj} \equiv h_j \, (\bar{v}_{kj}) \qquad\qquad \begin{matrix} k \in K \\ j \in J \end{matrix}$$

subject to:

(7.21) $$\sum_j x_{ij} \le k_i \, , \qquad\qquad i \in I$$

(7.22) $$\sum_i x_{ij} \ge \sum_k \bar{v}_{kj} \, \gamma_{kj} \, , \qquad\qquad j \in J$$

(7.23) $$\sum_k \gamma_{kj} = 1, \qquad\qquad j \in J$$

(7.24) $x_{ij}, \gamma_{kj} \geq 0,$ $i \epsilon I$
                                                                                      $j \epsilon J$
                                                                                      $k \epsilon K$

where

  K = set of grid points for approximating the area under the
        demand curve.

The criterion function (7.19) represents the area under the demand curve for all markets less the cost of shipping the products from the plants to the markets. In a more elaborate model, the criterion function would also include other terms for the cost of production. The market requirements constraint (7.22) requires that enough of the product be shipped from all the plants to meet demand, where demand is defined as was done in (7.14), that is, a convex combination of the grid points of demand.

This procedure can be extended to multiple products by using the procedures outlined in Duloy and Norton.[7] Also, it can be changed from a consumer-producer surplus maximization solution to a profit-maximizing scheme by specifying the criterion function as:

(7.25) $max\ R = pv - c(x),$

where

  p = price,
  v = demand, and
  x = production.

A comparison of (7.25) with (7.5) shows that the difference between the maximization of consumers' and producers' surplus and the maximization of profit is in the first term. In particular, for the case of a linear demand function, the first term becomes:

$$pv = (a + bv)v = av + bv^2,$$

which is the same as the area under the demand curve $h(v)$, except that in (7.8) the b coefficient is preceded by the number $\frac{1}{2}$.

In summary, the model in chapter 4 is limited because it employs fixed demand. Three schemes have been discussed here for modifying that limitation: (a) checking the prices that result from the model against the prices that were assumed initially to determine whether

7. Ibid.

they produce substantial changes in the demand requirements, in which case the model should be solved repeatedly until convergence is obtained; (b) setting up a consumers' and producers' surplus function, and maximizing it; or (c) setting up a profit-maximizing function and solving the resulting problem.

Since the previous work in this field has been content to use fixed demand and not to check on price consistency, there is as yet no experience with the use of any of the three methods. Research is underway to determine the convergence property of procedure (a) and to examine the economic implications of procedures (b) and (c).

No Substitution in Demand

The fixed-demand specification of the model also implies that no substitution is permitted between final products. In some cases, this limitation can be removed, that is, when demand requirements can be specified in units that can be supplied by various products. Examples are to be found in the fertilizer industry, in which demand requirements can be stated in terms of nutrients, or in the energy sector, in which demand requirements can be specified in terms of thermal units. In such cases, the model will select the products that will meet requirements at the lowest cost. For the fertilizer industry, this specification of demand was adopted by Stoutjesdijk, Frank, and Meeraus for their study of the East African fertilizer industry.[8] The final products in that model were a variety of specific phosphatic and nitrogenous fertilizers. The product requirements were specified, however, in terms of phosphorus and nitrogen nutrients. Since each fertilizer supplies one or both of these nutrients in fixed proportions, they were treated as substitutes in meeting the nutrient requirements.

More frequently, however, one encounters a set of final products with no substitution permitted. If the level of aggregation is high and only a few final products are specified, then substitution between products may be so difficult that fixed demands occur in practice.

8. Ardy Stoutjesdijk, Charles Frank, Jr., and Alexander Meeraus, "Planning in the Chemical Sector," in *Industrial Investment Analysis under Increasing Returns*, eds. Stoutjesdijk and Larry E. Westphal (forthcoming).

For example, if the final products in a forest and forest industries study are specified as lumber, linerboard, kraft paper, and newsprint, then little substitution could occur between the products. If, however, the breakdown of final products is so fine that it includes several classes of lumber, then it would be very important to permit substitution between products.

Substitution can be incorporated into the model by using the consumer-producer surplus maximization method described above. In this case, however, the demand functions should be specified so as to permit substitution.

Prices of Some Inputs and Outputs Fixed

The model described above assumes that the prices of domestic raw materials, imports, exports, and by-products are fixed. This is a satisfactory assumption so long as changes in the level of inputs or outputs to or from the industry under study do not result in substantial changes in these prices. For example, purchases of sulfuric acid on the world market by a pulp and paper mill will not noticeably affect world market prices of sulfuric acid. Similarly, the exports of lumber from a single sawmill are not likely to be of sufficient volume to affect world prices. On the other hand, local purchase of lumber by a pulp and paper mill might be of sufficient volume to affect the cost of lumber locally. When this latter case occurs, one can make a relatively small change to the model, and thereby incorporate the price variation into the model. This would be done in the lumber example by adding several variables for purchasing lumber. Each variable would have associated with it a different price for lumber and each variable would be bounded from above. Also, an additional balance constraint would be written setting total lumber purchases equal to the sum of lumber purchased through each of the variables. Then, when the model is solved, lumber would be purchased first via the least costly activity. If demand exceeded the upper bound on this variable, then the next cheapest activity would be used, and so on. In this manner, an increasing marginal cost supply function for lumber can be built into the model. An analogous procedure can be used for exports or by-product prices, except that sales would be specified with declining marginal prices.

No Uncertainty

Any expansion of industrial capacity involves substantial uncertainties. The models of this volume are useful for studying the effect of "large event" uncertainty but not "small event" uncertainty. Large event uncertainty refers to events that are small in number but that could have a large effect on the investment projects under study. In a company model, such an event might be whether or not a competitor chooses to build a plant at a certain location. In a regional model, a large event would be the decision of one of the large countries not to participate in a common market agreement. The effects of these kinds of uncertainty can be studied with the models discussed in this volume by solving the model repeatedly and including or excluding variables representing the various possible large events. For example, in the regional study, the model would be solved with and without the participation of the particular country.

On the other hand, the models do not include a systematic treatment of small event uncertainty, such as uncertainty about future demand or about future prices. In order to include such phenomena, it would be necessary to specify market requirements and prices as random variables, and the model would have to be solved as a stochastic linear mixed-integer programming problem. Though methods of solving such problems have not yet been investigated fully, it is anticipated that such methods will require large amounts of computer time.

Representation of Policy Objectives

The decisionmakers who are charged with responsibility for project design and selection will usually have a criterion function that is very complex. It may include the number of votes or the political influence to be gained or lost from making a specific choice, the income distribution effects of the choice, the employment effects, the effects of the choice on the decisionmakers' personal income and wealth, the appearance and technical quality of the plant, environmental considerations, and so forth. No pretense is made here about the ability of this or any other model to capture all of the complexities of a decision under preferences.

The model may make it possible to provide information to the decisionmaker about income distribution, employment, and environmental effects at less cost than in the absence of the model. It cannot, however, include the decisionmaker's complete utility function or preference orderings. Therefore, the modeling effort must be viewed as only a part of the overall project design and selection problem.

Size of the Programming Problem

The model can become a large computational problem even for a relatively modest number of plants, markets, and products. For example, a model of the West African steel industry with 5 plants, 28 markets, 11 productive units, 3 time periods, 7 final products, 6 intermediate products, and 19 raw material and labor inputs had about 1,500 constraints and 5,000 variables.[9] When the investment variables y are allowed to vary continuously between 0 and 1 rather than being restricted to the integer values 0 or 1, the model is a linear program rather than a mixed-integer program. In this case, the model can be solved on a large computer in a few minutes; it is time consuming and tedious, however, to check the input and output in order to be certain that no errors occurred in model specification or data input.

When the investment variables are restricted to take on the values 0 or 1 only, the size and complexity of the computational problem is greatly increased. This is not so much a limitation of the model itself, however, as a limitation in the state of the art of computational techniques. Chapter 8 explicitly addresses this aspect of the project selection model.

Conclusion

After reading the above list of limitations of the model, the reader undoubtedly realizes the importance of proceeding with caution.

9. David Kendrick and Alex Meeraus, "A Model of the West African Steel Industry" (Development Research Center, World Bank, Washington, D.C., 1974; processed).

Nevertheless, we believe that it is most important to proceed. As algorithms, computer codes, and methods of economic analysis improve in the future, many of these limitations will be decreased in importance. For the moment, however, the models discussed in this book represent the best tradeoff we have been able to devise between the quality of model specification and the difficulty of computation.

8

Solution Methods

PROCEDURES DESCRIBED IN THIS CHAPTER can be adopted to obtain explicit solutions to the models presented in this volume. Several classes of computer codes have been formulated to deal with the mixed-integer programming problem; the only proven codes offered by the major computer manufacturers and software houses at the present time, however, are enumerative-type algorithms, with "branch and bound" the most commonly used method.

The description of the implicit enumeration method and of the procedures underlying branch and bound is kept at an intuitive level, in the sense that no formal mathematical statement of the solution procedure is given. Rather, the description is aimed at giving an impression of the problems associated with obtaining explicit solutions to these models.[1]

Although efforts are made to produce better methods for solving mixed-integer programming problems, it is probable that branch and bound methods will remain the most often used solution methods for large-scale mixed-integer programming problems. Because of the relative inefficiency of the code, the size of the models that can be solved

---

This chapter borrows liberally from: Alexander Meeraus and Ardy Stoutjesdijk, "The Solution Procedure for FERTILEA," in *Industrial Investment Analysis under Increasing Returns,* eds. Stoutjesdijk and Larry E. Westphal (forthcoming).

1. For more complete statements on the general-purpose codes, the reader is referred to A. M. Geoffrion and R. E. Marsten, "Integer Programming Algorithms: A Framework and State-of-the-Art Survey," in *Perspectives on Optimization*, ed. Geoffrion (Reading, Mass.: Addison-Wesley, 1972).

at reasonable cost is fairly limited. Also, in some cases, the models described here might be applied in circumstances in which no easy access to large-scale computers exists. For these reasons, this chapter includes a description of a number of hand calculations that may (a) reduce the size of the model to a more manageable dimension, and (b) enable an insight into the structure of the planning problem that may aid the project planner even if the model is not fully solved.[2] Additional project- or sector-specific shortcuts are often possible, and they will be described in later volumes.

General-Purpose Computer Codes

Before describing the methods of implicit enumeration and branch and bound, it will be useful to restate the nature of the computational problem associated with the class of models presented in this volume. The variables in the model belong to two groups: one consists of variables that can take on the values of 0 and 1 only (the y's); the other consists of variables that are permitted to assume any nonnegative value. The presence of integer variables converts the optimizing models in this volume from linear programming problems to mixed-integer linear programming problems. The solution of models of this type is greatly complicated by the large number of combinations of 0–1 variables (project combinations) that are normally possible; if n stands for the number of possible projects or project variants, the total number of possible project combinations is equal to 2^n. For example, in the case of a problem involving three integer variables—y_1, y_2, and y_3—the following combinations of values for these variables are possible:

y_1	y_2	y_3
0	0	0
0	0	1
0	1	0
0	1	1
1	0	0
1	0	1
1	1	0
1	1	1

2. The feasibility of doing relatively complex hand calculations has increased rapidly in recent years with the advent of low-cost but sophisticated hand calculators, including the programmable variety.

Enumeration

This solution method is based on the fact that a mixed-integer programming problem consists of a number of implicit linear programming problems, one for each combination of 0–1 variables. Solving each linear programming problem separately and ranking the solutions in terms of objective function value enables the identification of the optimal mixed-integer programming solution. This method is practicable, of course, only if the number of possible combinations of 0–1 variables is relatively small, as in the case cited above, in which eight linear programs would have to be solved.

Branch and bound

The method of branch and bound is based on the circumstance that not all possible project combinations need to be evaluated to find the least-cost set of projects. In fact, the branch and bound procedure frequently enables the rejection of a large number of project combinations before they have been explicitly evaluated.

The solution procedure in branch and bound is the following. First, the mixed-integer programming problem is transformed into an ordinary linear programming problem by relaxing all of the integer conditions: that is, all integer variables are permitted to take on non-integer values. This means that, in an integer problem of the 0–1 type, the integer variables can assume any value between and including 0 and 1. Normally, it can be expected that, in the optimal solution to the relaxed mixed-integer problem, most of the 0–1 variables have a fractional value, although sometimes they turn out to have values that are very close to 0 or 1, if not 0 or 1. In such cases, it is not necessary to carry out further computational work, and the integer problem can be qualified as solved. In the large majority of cases, however, it will be necessary to continue the optimization process. The major problem now is what procedure to adopt to identify a solution that satisfies all constraints, including the integrality conditions.

This procedure can be explained conveniently by making use of the concept of a binary tree. Assume a problem that involves three 0–1 variables; the binary tree is then as given in figure 7.

Each juncture of the tree is called a node. Node 0 is the starting point of the search procedure for the least-cost combination of 0–1 variables. At node 0, all 0–1 variables are permitted to assume frac-

Figure 7. The Binary Tree

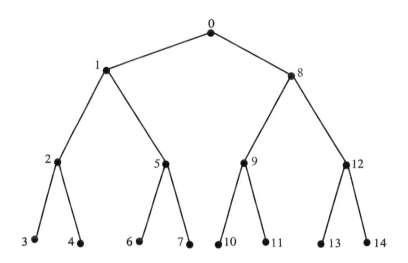

tional values, and the integrality conditions are therefore completely relaxed. Going down the tree, different integer variables are then placed at either 0 or 1; all remaining integer variables are permitted to assume fractional values. At node 1, one integer variable, say y_1, is set to an integer value, while all others continue to be permitted to have fractional values. At node 2, a second integer variable, say y_2, is set to 0 or 1, and all integer variables except y_1 and y_2 are permitted to assume fractional values, and so forth.

The binary tree in figure 7 is fully developed, and it illustrates the case in which all nodes need to be evaluated to identify the least-cost solution to the problem. It should be noted that, if this were necessary, the method of branch and bound would be less efficient than that of implicit enumeration, because in the latter case only nodes 7 to 14 would be evaluated.[3] The number of nodes is considerably larger than the number of 0–1 combinations because the nodes include problems with integer variables at fractional values. In fact, the number of nodes is equal to $2^{n+1} - 1$, as compared with the number of 0–1 combinations of 2^n, where n is the number of integer variables.

3. Nodes 7 to 14 are the only ones where all integer variables are at either 0 or 1.

The method of branch and bound, however, is based on the fact that in most cases only a fraction of the nodes needs to be evaluated; also, it takes less computer time to solve a successive number of nodes than a similar number of linear programming problems.

The problem is specified in figure 8, which includes three integer variables, y_1, y_2, and y_3. The value of the objective function is denoted by x_0; integer variables are placed at the value 0 in the southwest direction, and at 1 in the southeast direction. At node 0, it is decided to place the fractional "integer variable" y_2 at the value 1, and the objective function turns out to have a value of, say, 90.

The problem at node 1 is identical to that at node 0, except that variable y_2 is preset to 1; this involves an additional cost of 10 in objective function value.[4] On the basis of information revealed by the optimal solution to problem 1 (to be explained momentarily), it is decided to place one of the remaining integer variables, y_3, at 0, thus creating problem 2. An objective function value of 95 is obtained, but since the one remaining integer variable, y_1, is not an integer value, unlike y_2 (which is 1) and y_3 (which is 0), this solution cannot be qualified as an integer solution, and the next problem is created. This is problem 3, with y_1 fixed at 0. This combination of values for the 0–1 variables appears to render solution of the problem infeasible: that is, it is impossible to satisfy all constraints.

In order to continue the search for the global optimum, it is necessary to go up the tree, a process that is called "backtracking." To create problem 3, decisions were necessary at nodes 0, 1, and 2 regarding the direction into which to set the fractional integer variables. Problems that are created by placing the integer variable at the alternative value are on the "waiting list," and the relevant nodes are referred to as "hanging nodes." At this point, three problems are on the waiting list—problems 4, 5, and 6.

Assume that it is decided that problem 4 should be created first. As long as a feasible solution to this problem can be obtained, this solution must be an integer solution. In the example, this is the case, with $x_0 = 105$. The search for the least-cost solution cannot be stopped here, however, because other integer solutions may exist with

---

4. It is an essential consequence of adding constraints to an optimization problem that the cost of the program increases (or, that the benefits of the program decrease); since, at node 0, y_2 did not come out at 1 (although permitted to do so), it was clearly not the optimal value of this variable.

Figure 8. The Method of Branch and Bound

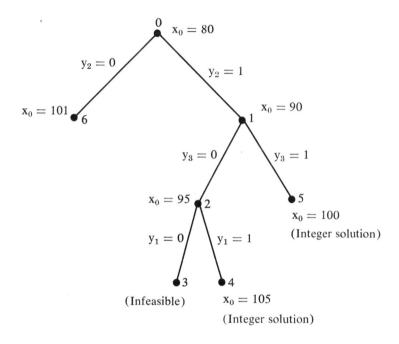

a lower (and therefore better, at least in a minimization problem) value of x_0. Of the two remaining problems on the waiting list, problem 5 is solved first. Once more an integer solution is found, and it represents an improvement on the previously identified integer solution, which can now at once be qualified as a "local optimum solution." Problem 6, the last remaining problem on the waiting list, is now developed. A linear programming solution to this problem is found, but the value of x_0 is higher than the one found for problem 5.

Now, advantage can be taken of the fact that the solution to a descending problem is always worse than the solution of the problem it originated from, and the search for integer solutions that could be developed from node 6 can be abandoned. This process is also referred to as "bounding." The search for a better integer solution in the hypothetical problem can therefore legitimately be stopped, and the solution to problem 5 is declared the "global optimum solution."

The efficiency of the method of branch and bound depends crucially on the procedure that is used to determine the priority by which integer variables are set to either 0 or 1. Although available solution procedures vary as far as the solution strategy is concerned, they all make use of the cost information (that is, the shadow prices) that is contained in the linear programming solution to the problem at every node. Generally, the search strategy is based on the estimated change in the value of the objective function as a result of setting one of the integer variables to either 0 or 1, leaving all other 0–1 variables free to assume any fractional value. This estimate is made for each integer variable separately, as long as it has a fractional value in the optimal solution to the relaxed problem. On the basis of this estimate, several strategies suggest themselves. One is to select the integer variable that, if placed at either 0 or 1, causes the smallest deterioration in the value of the objective function for the linear programming problem (assuming cost minimization). Another strategy is to select the integer variable that, if placed at either 0 or 1, causes the largest deterioration in the value of the objective function for the relaxed problem, and to set its value in the opposite direction. These possible strategies may sometimes be complemented by special instructions relating to how far the search has progressed in a given direction or to the priorities that can logically be set in the planning problem.

Several matters should be stressed at this point. The procedure outlined above is designed to set priorities in terms of which 0–1 variables should be placed at an integer value first and whether that value should be 0 or 1. A second point that needs emphasis is that the direction of the search for the optimal solution is decided upon by an investigation of a single 0–1 variable at a time, whereas all other integer variables remain either fixed or relaxed. Because the investigation is restricted to one integer variable, the direction chosen in branch and bound is often incorrect, and frequently it appears necessary to return to an integer variable that was initially set to a value that caused the smallest deterioration in the objective function value and to place its value the opposite way. For this reason, branch and bound has often been found an inefficient solution procedure to identify the global optimum solution to a mixed-integer problem of anything except a very limited size. Nevertheless, branch and bound is the solution procedure that is used most often for the class of problems dealt with in this volume. There are essentially two reasons for this: (a) other solution procedures are often even less efficient, and

(b) the branch and bound method is frequently very efficient in the identification of local optimum solutions. The use of branch and bound for this purpose deserves further discussion.

The solution of the completely relaxed problem at node 0 gives a lower value of the objective function (in a minimization problem) than any subsequently generated problem in the binary tree. The global optimum solution will have an objective function value that is closest to the completely relaxed problem, even though it must always be higher (except in the unlikely case in which the completely relaxed problem yields a solution with all integer variables at integer values, in which case it is the global optimum solution to the model). Given this knowledge, the quality of any integer solution can be approximated by comparing its objective function value with that of the completely relaxed problem. If the difference between the two is only a few percentage points, it is often unnecessary to proceed with the search for the proven global optimum solution. In many cases in which planning problems have been cast in the form of a mixed-integer programming framework, the analyst has adopted this procedure. In such cases, it is essential that the results be clearly qualified as local optimum results.

Two avenues are open to improve the procedures to obtain global optimum solutions to mixed-integer programming models. One is to take advantage of the special structure many planning problems have, and to incorporate these features explicitly into the computer code. Another possibility is to attempt to narrow down the optimization problem by performing a number of calculations (with or without a computer) on aspects of the problem, in the hope that a less complex problem needs to be solved on the basis of a general-purpose computer code. Several such calculations, referred to as hand calculations, are described in the next section.

Hand Calculations

A number of calculations can be carried out before the automated solution of the model by computer; they are aimed at eliminating projects or project combinations from among the set of feasible alternatives. To some extent, the computer can be helpful in carrying out these calculations, but the availability of a computer is not essential. Moreover, the calculations can be performed by a much smaller computer than would be required for the solution of a medium- to large-scale project selection model. The hand calculations can therefore be particularly useful in circumstances in which no easy access to large-scale computers exists. To what extent a reasonable approximation to the most attractive project combination can be made without a computer depends largely on the complexity of the project selection problem. It should be obvious that in the case of a static, one-product, single-location model, the solution of the model can be obtained by static break-even analysis without help from the computer; such problems are not treated here because they are unlikely to occur. Generally, what will be said below applies to the complete project selection model that is designed to determine size, time-phasing, and location of new capacity.

The hand calculations are described in the following sequence. First, it is indicated how potential projects can be eliminated on the basis of a comparison between import cost and marginal cost of domestic production. In a spatially disaggregated model, it is shown how specific locations can be eliminated from the choice set. For all remaining possible project combinations, the analysis is carried one step further, and a procedure is described that permits the further elimination of projects on the basis of a comparison of import cost and "augmented marginal cost." The latter include the marginal cost of production, augmented by other cost elements computed at their minimum level. Among other things, the computation of the augmented marginal cost requires the determination of the maximum excess capacity that could be constructed during the planning period. Finally, attention is paid to the introduction of mutual exclusivity constraints.

Marginal costs versus import costs

Frequently, the c.i.f. import price of a commodity, or its projected level, is the benchmark that is used to determine whether or not that commodity should be produced domestically. Commonly, the comparison is made on the basis of the estimated average cost of production of the commodity in the country concerned. In the presence of economies of scale and interdependencies with other productive activities, this comparison may lead to incorrect decisions. The following example is designed to demonstrate simultaneously the importance of interdependence and the danger associated with using average cost of production as a signal regarding the desirability of domestic production.

Assume that the production of a given consumption good, denoted

Table 2. Domestic Production Compared with Imports:
Some Hypothetical Data

Production factors	Product A	Product B	Product C
Market requirements	1,000 units	1,000 units	—
Import price	$10.50 per unit	$15.50 per unit	—
Intermediate use of C	0.8 per unit	0.4 per unit	—
Import price of C	$5.00 per unit	$5.00 per unit	—
Domestic production cost			
with imported C	$11.00 per unit	$16.00 per unit	—
Domestic production cost of C			
At output level of			
400 units	—	—	$5.50 per unit
At output level of			
800 units	—	—	$4.50 per unit
At output level of			
1,200 units	—	—	$4.00 per unit

— = not applicable.

by A, is contemplated. Product A requires the input of intermediate product C, which is produced under strong economies of scale. Independently, an investigation is conducted into the feasibility of starting the production of consumption good B, which also requires a quantity of C as intermediate input. Table 2 contains some hypothetical information on market requirements, import prices, and domestic production cost for commodities A, B, and C. The following project combinations may be considered:

- The production of A alone, on the basis of imported C. This project is to be rejected because the domestic production cost of A is higher than the import cost ($11.00 versus $10.50).
- The production of A as well as C. This project combination is also unattractive because, at the required output level of C, its domestic supply price of $4.50 results in a domestic production cost of A of $10.60 ($7.00 + 0.8 × $4.50), which is higher than the import price of A ($10.50).
- The production of B alone, on the basis of imported C. This project is to be rejected because the domestic production cost of B is higher than the import price ($16.00 as against $15.50).
- The production of B on the basis of domestically produced C. This project should be rejected because the domestic production cost of B is higher than the import price ($16.20 as against $15.50).

- The production of A and B on the basis of domestically produced C. This project combination is attractive because it leads to total net savings compared with imports. At the required output level of 1,200 units of C, the domestic production cost of C is $4.00 per unit. This permits the domestic production of A at a cost of $10.20 per unit ($7.00 + 0.8 × $4.00), resulting in savings of $300 over imports of 1,000 ($10,200 as against $10,500). At a cost of $4.00 per unit of C, production of B is possible at a cost per unit of $15.60 ($14.00 + 0.4 × $4.00). Although this is still higher than the import price of $15.50, the loss associated with the domestic production of 1,000 units of B is only $100, compared with a gain of $300 made possible by the domestic production of A. The net gain to be derived from the entire program is therefore $200.

Two points are illustrated by this deceptively simple example. First, the explicit consideration of interdependencies among projects may have a considerable effect on the cost structure of some or all of the projects under consideration. Given the frequent occurrence of interdependence, on the one hand, and the rapidly increasing number of possible project combinations, on the other hand, a systematic analytical scheme, susceptible to computerized search procedures, is required to carry out the selection of the least-cost project combination. Second, individual projects may not be rejected routinely just because the estimated average cost of production is higher than the import price, because this procedure would neglect the possible beneficial indirect effects of the project on other, related projects. The project selection models proposed in this volume enable the quantification of such effects.

It can be proven that the only valid comparison that may be made with c.i.f. import prices, for activities that exhibit economies of scale or for those that are technically linked with activities that are subject to economies of scale, is on the basis of marginal cost of domestic production.[5] Whenever marginal cost of production is higher than the import price, domestic production is inefficient under any cir-

---

5. For a formal proof of this screening rule, see Larry E. Westphal and Yung Rhee "Single Process Models," in *Industrial Investment Analysis under Increasing Returns,* eds. Stoutjesdijk and Westphal (forthcoming); for detailed directions on how to calculate the marginal cost of production for an interdependent set of production activities, see the User's Guide in this series of volumes.

cumstances. If marginal cost is lower, domestic production may be attractive, depending on the magnitude of the other cost elements, and the cost effects that the project has on other, interdependent activities.

Interdependence among productive activities is by no means a trivial matter, but is in fact a basic characteristic of the economic system. It is only as a result of major advances in computer technology in recent years that such interdependencies may now be represented systematically and analyzed quantitatively at the microeconomic level.

The effectiveness of the marginal cost rule varies, but in many cases it may permit the elimination of several productive activities from the planning problem, thus simplifying the solution of the model. In other cases, however, it may be desirable to narrow the choice set further, and the logical next step appears to be an analysis of other cost elements that might legitimately be added to the marginal cost of domestic production, so that a further elimination of production possibilities can be achieved.

Marginal cost and transport cost

If demand is regionally specified, it may be possible to eliminate potential production locations from the planning problem by an analysis of c.i.f. import cost, marginal production cost at each plant site, and transport cost from each possible origin to each possible destination. If domestic production at one location is compared with imports, the reasoning can be as follows: if the marginal cost of production per unit of product (that is, the costs of materials and other current inputs, which are assumed to be constant), augmented by transportation cost to a specific marketing center, is higher than the c.i.f. import price plus transport cost from the importing point to the marketing center, the marketing center will not be supplied from the producing location under consideration because the addition of the capital cost would only further tip the scales in favor of the imports.

If production at more than one location is considered, a similar comparison of delivered marginal cost can be made from each producing location to each demand center. If many sites and marketing centers are considered, this phase in the hand calculations may be very cumbersome, and a small desk computer, or time-sharing terminal, would be useful. In the worst case, the comparison of delivered marginal cost can be skipped, although then elimination of producing sites with a severe transport cost disadvantage in relation to alternative sources would not be possible. In addition, as will be discussed in the next section, it would not permit the determination of the largest potential marketing area for each producing location, which is of importance in the computation of the maximum plant scale.

Maximum plant scales

Since the demand for final products in the project selection model is postulated exogenously, maximum plant scales for final products can be determined if the maximum amount of excess capacity for each plant can be established, taking into account the technical restrictions imposed on plant scales. Once maximum plant scales for final products have been determined, similar plant scales for intermediate products can be computed, if the various forms of interdependence are taken into account and, once more, if maximum excess capacity can be established.

To determine the maximum level of excess capacity in final product plants, it is necessary to start with the projection of final demand, both domestic and export, for the planning period. As long as there is no substitution among products, the determination of maximum demand for each product, and for each time period, is not difficult. If demand does not decrease over time, the maximum final demand for each product is equal to final demand in the last planning period, augmented by the estimated exports in that period. This maximum demand level is also the maximum plant size that needs to be considered because it would not pay to construct overcapacity in the last planning period of the model: it would imply higher investment cost at no benefit during the model's planning period. Assuming that each final product that is not eliminated on the basis of the marginal cost rule is produced domestically at the maximum demand level, the demand level for all intermediate products and raw materials can be calculated with the use of the input-output coefficients.

If demand is regionally specified, so that transport cost is important, a tighter estimate of maximum final demand for each product in the model from each potential production location can be made by comparing domestic delivered marginal cost to each region from a potential producing location with that from the importing point. Whenever delivered cost from an alternative source is lower than that from a specific producing location, the latter is eliminated as a source of supply for the region in question. For that location, therefore, the maximum demand to be considered should exclude the demand from this demand region. This exercise should be carried out for each product and for each producing location.

The determination of the maximum plant size for other than the final period in the planning model is slightly more complicated because it may be efficient to construct excess capacity in the presence of economies of scale. It is possible, however, to indicate the maximum excess capacity that could be constructed efficiently. Assume that, in a given period, a specific level of output can be provided by two plants of capacity h_1 and h_2, respectively, with the construction of h_2 and h_1 separated by a period of n years. Alternatively, one plant of capacity $h_1 + h_2$ can be constructed. Using the linear construction cost function, the construction of a single plant is to be preferred only if the following inequality holds[6]:

$$\omega + v\,(h_1 + h_2) < \omega + v \cdot h_1 + (\omega + v \cdot h_2)\,(1 + \rho)^{-n}$$

where

ω = fixed-charge portion of investment costs,
v = slope of linear portion of investment cost function,
ρ = the discount rate.

The model may be specified in terms of subperiods of more than one year each; n is the total number of years. The inequality is valid only if, in each subperiod, construction of new capacity can take place, and if demand is a constant average within each subperiod, although increasing from subperiod to subperiod. In other words, demand is specified as a step function—as, for example, in figure 9.

In the figure, *OSUV* is the "true" growth path of demand, and *OPTRW* is the stepwise approximation, so that *OP* is the average demand level for period 1, and *OQ* the level for period 2. Then, $OP = h_1$, and $PQ = h_2$. The inequality states that a single plant will be constructed only if the construction cost in the earlier period for a capacity of $h_1 + h_2$ is less than the sum of the cost of constructing the smaller capacity h_1 and the discounted cost of building the addi-

---

6. The complication caused by the presence of capacity-related recurrent costs is disregarded.

Figure 9. The Demand Specification for the Calculation of
Excess Capacity

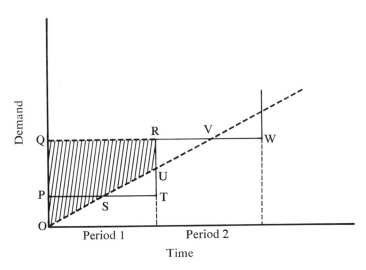

tional capacity h_2 a period of n years later. As can be seen from
figure 9, the amount of excess capacity during the first period is
approximately equal to h_2, since the area OPS is about equal to the
area STU.[7]

From the inequality, it follows that excess capacity, χ, will be constructed as long as:

$$\chi \leq \frac{\omega}{\nu[(1 + \rho)^n - 1]} .$$

The maximum excess capacity that will be constructed is then equal
to:

$$\chi = h_2 = \frac{1}{(1 + \rho)^n - 1} \cdot \frac{\omega}{\nu} ,$$

that is, when the cost of the larger plant is exactly equal to the total
cost of the χ of smaller plant h_1 plus the discounted cost of the later

7. This is an approximation, the closeness of which depends on the true
growth path of demand.

Table 3. Typical Values for $\dfrac{1}{(1+\rho)^n - 1}$

n	$\rho = 0.05$	$\rho = 0.10$	$\rho = 0.15$
$n = 1$	20.00	10.00	6.67
$n = 2$	9.76	4.76	3.10
$n = 3$	6.34	3.02	1.92
$n = 4$	4.64	2.15	1.34
$n = 5$	3.62	1.64	0.99

plant h_2. Two separate plants h_1 and h_2 will be preferred on cost considerations, if:

$$h_2 > \frac{1}{(1+\rho)^n - 1} \cdot \frac{\omega}{v}.$$

Some typical values for $\dfrac{1}{(1+\rho)^n - 1}$ are given in Table 3. Given that ω/v is a constant for any specific productive unit, the larger the discount rate or the number of years apart that plants can be built, the smaller the excess capacity it would be efficient to construct.[8]

Augmented marginal costs

Given the information on the fixed (ω) and variable (v) charges on construction, the discount rate (ρ), and the length of each time period in the model, maximum excess capacity for the production of each commodity in the model, at each site, and for each time period can be computed. Augmenting the maximum demand estimates previously computed with the maximum excess capacity for each productive unit results in upper bounds on productive units, for each time period and for each product.

Elimination of production possibilities can now take place on the basis of the following procedure. Starting with the raw materials, all inputs into successive stages of production are valued at the lowest possible delivered marginal cost. The origin of each input may thus be either imports from abroad or one of the possible domestic supply

---

8. The calculation of the maximum excess capacity as described here is in the same vein as Alan Manne's optimal cycling time. The interested reader is referred to A. S. Manne, ed., *Investments for Capacity Expansion: Size, Location and Time-Phasing* (Cambridge, Mass.: The M.I.T. Press, 1967).

centers. Eventually, this exercise yields the accumulated marginal cost of production of final products at each site. Those production possibilities that have higher accumulated marginal cost of production than the imported product, delivered at the plant site, can be eliminated. Then, the marginal cost of production can be augmented by the annualized construction cost per unit of product for the maximum plant scale, taking into account maximum demand as well as maximum excess capacity, and assuming full capacity utilization. These costs are referred to as augmented marginal cost; they differ from average costs because they do not include construction cost charges for any of the preceding production phases. The elimination rule is now that whenever a production unit has augmented marginal cost that exceeds the c.i.f. import price plus transport cost to the plant site, the production activity can legitimately be deleted from the choice set.

The two reasons given earlier for making a straightforward comparison between average costs and import prices illegitimate—that is, capacity sharing and differential cost pricing over time—have been neutralized. The effect of production cost of capacity sharing has been taken at its extreme by considering only marginal cost of production for intermediate inputs: it is implicitly assumed that the fixed charge is carried entirely by other interdependent activities. Consequently, the estimate of domestic production costs, as it is used for elimination purposes, is likely to be an underestimate. Similarly, by calculating the production cost at the maximum scale of the productive unit, including maximum excess capacity, and at full capacity utilization, no further scope for differential marginal cost pricing over time exists: if augmented marginal cost calculated under these most favorable conditions cannot be covered, the activity can never be optimal. Finally, gains in distribution cost cannot change the results because the import costs with which the production costs are being compared are taken at their most unfavorable level—that is, at the plant site, and including transport cost from the importing point to the production location. In conclusion, therefore, the elimination procedure is legitimate because it compares domestic production cost at a given plant site at their most favorable level with supply cost from alternative sources at their most unfavorable level.

The above comparison can be made for each possible production location in the model. It can also be carried out for each time period, although it is preferable to start with the last time period. As long as demand is growing over time, and as long as there are economies of scale in production, if a production activity can be eliminated for the last period in the model, it can also be eliminated for all preceding periods.

After those productive units that have higher augmented marginal cost than import cost plus transport cost to the plant site have been eliminated, the maximum demand estimates for intermediate products may require revision. Subsequently, the augmented marginal cost for the most advanced intermediate products—those products which are direct inputs into final products as opposed to those which are used in the production of higher order intermediate products—can be compared with the c.i.f. price of imported equivalents delivered to the plant site, whereupon a similar elimination can take place as was described in the case of final products. Again, the augmented marginal cost is based on the accumulated marginal cost of production of the intermediate product under consideration, and on valuing the average fixed cost per unit at the maximum plant scale and at full capacity utilization. If intermediate productive units can be eliminated on this basis, it will be necessary to investigate the implications of this elimination on the cost structure of the final products, since the hitherto used marginal cost of assumed domestic production of the intermediate product must be replaced by the import price of the intermediate plus transport cost to the plant. In certain cases, this may lead to eliminating the final product as well.

A number of iterations may therefore be required before the elimination procedure on the basis of augmented marginal cost is completed. The aid of a small computer could simplify this phase in the hand calculations considerably; for this reason, the User's Guide to this series of volumes contains instructions and examples of simple computer programs that can be used for this purpose.

Mutual exclusivity constraints

Mutual exclusivity constraints impose bounds on the sum of a set of 0–1 variables or, in other words, on the number of productive units to be installed.[9] For example, if one plant can in principle be con-

9. The use of mutual exclusivity constraints of this sort in mixed-integer programming was suggested by Alan Manne and Richard Inman; they used the idea successfully in the IPE algorithm for mixed-integer programming. See A. S. Manne, "A Mixed Integer Algorithm for Project Evaluation," in *Multi-Level Planning: Case Studies in Mexico*, eds. Louis M. Goreux and Manne (Amsterdam: North-Holland/American Elsevier, 1973), chapter VI.

structed in each of five time periods, but it can be demonstrated that in practice no more than two plants will be built, a mutual exclusivity constraint of the following form can be added to the model specification:

$$\sum_{\tau=1}^{5} y_{mit} \leq 2.$$

Constraints of this nature may be of substantial help in the identification of the optimal solution to the model.

Of course, there is a link between the maximum excess capacity and the maximum number of plants that could optimally be built during the planning period. Given specified levels of demand for each productive unit, for each period, the maximum plant scale can be determined, as was shown above. Once the maximum plant scale is determined, it is possible to derive the maximum number of plants that can optimally be built during the planning period. The procedure can be demonstrated by a numerical example. Demand for product A is 5,000 tons in period 1, and it increases to 11,000 tons in period 2. Apart from the problem of gestation periods, a decision must be made about whether one plant of 11,000 tons is to be preferred, or whether two separate plants should be built, one period of three years apart. Clearly, the construction of a single plant would result in an initial excess capacity of 6,000 tons.

The condition under which one plant with excess capacity will be preferred to two plants can be stated as follows:

$$h_2 \leq \frac{1}{(1 + \rho)^n - 1} \cdot \frac{\omega}{\nu}$$

or

$$h_2 \{(1 + \rho)^n - 1\} \leq \frac{\omega}{\nu}.$$

With h_2 equal to 6,000, and $(1 + \rho)^n - 1$ equal to 0.331, one plant will be preferred as long as ω/ν does not exceed 1,986. Assuming that in the example it does not, the maximum number of plants that will be built is equal to 1, in which case the following mutual exclusivity constraint can be added to the model:

$$y_{mi1} + y_{mi2} \leq 1.$$

Special problems

The structure of the planning problem may be so complex that the above hand calculations need to be modified. First, their implementation by hand may be too cumbersome. In that case, simple computer programs may be written for use on small computers so that the analyst can carry out some or all of the calculations. The User's Guide in this series gives specific instructions on how to proceed in such cases.

Second, special complications may occur that require modification of the procedures just outlined. One complication that may frequently occur is product substitution. In that case, the hand calculations become considerably more difficult to perform. For example, in the fertilizer industry several products may provide the same nutrient, and final demand is specified by nutrient. This complication affects in particular the determination of maximum plant scales, because the elimination of one final product directly affects the maximum plant scale of a competitive product. The appropriate procedure to adopt in such cases is to determine the maximum plant for each product by estimating maximum final demand at the minimum supply level of competitive products, and adding maximum excess capacity computed as before. Unless specific minimum supply levels for each product are specified, this minimum supply level of competitive products is zero. It is important to realize that maximum plant sizes for intermediates depend on which final products are retained in the production plan. In the case of substitutable products, therefore, generally more elimination rounds are required than for other products.

Problem-specific hand calculations

The procedures described so far are more or less generally applicable for investment planning problems that are susceptible to the project selection model specification. In addition, a large number of problem-specific decision rules that simplify the solution of a given model can often be identified. One of the purposes of the description of possible hand calculations is to demonstrate how such calculations can be designed and performed, and to what extent they enable a narrowing of the choice set open to the project analyst.

Alternative Solutions

Generally, obtaining the global optimum solution to the project selection model is desirable, because it provides a benchmark to determine the tradeoffs between the least-cost investment program and alternative programs that may be preferred for various reasons. It may not always be possible, however, to obtain the global optimum solution at reasonable cost. Given the state of the art, this situation will be fairly common for project selection problems in which the number of 0–1 variables is greater than 100. Moreover, if the hand calculations prove ineffective in eliminating productive activities, the project analyst may have to use the model as a device for calculating the cost of alternative solutions. In that case, a number of decisions are made with respect to the planning problem on the basis of insight, intuition, known or suspected political constraints, and so forth, and the implications of these decisions are assessed on the basis of a solution of the model for the remaining undetermined variables. Depending on how costly the solution of the partially fixed model is, a varying number of solutions may be obtained for alternative decisions; they frequently yield a good insight into the structure of the planning problem at hand.

In practice, so far, simulation has proved to be an extremely valuable tool for project selection, even to the extent that analysts have focused on this use exclusively in several instances. It is particularly helpful in case the planning problem is complicated by constraints that do not lend themselves easily to modeling, as was indicated in chapter 6.

Conclusion

The solution of project selection models incorporating economies of scale is difficult and costly, particularly if the model is of medium to large size. The global optimum solution should frequently not be considered attainable for the larger models. Computational techniques are rapidly improving, however, and the great progress that has been achieved during the last decade gives reason for optimism.

Good solutions to project selection models can now be obtained at very reasonable cost, frequently permitting substantial improvement in the quality of sectoral investment programs. Moreover, careful analysis of the problem under consideration may often permit substantial simplification of the decision problem, leading to savings in computer time, as well as valuable insight into the structure of the problem. Finally, the use of the project selection model is increasingly recognized as a tool for simulation; in the extreme case it eliminates the need for a complete solution of the model.

9

Summary and Conclusions

THE WIDESPREAD AVAILABILITY OF ELECTRONIC COMPUTERS—from tiny, handheld calculators to giant number crunchers—is producing a revolution in methods of doing project analysis and investment planning. Previously, rate-of-return calculations could be performed for only a few variants of a project, and it was extremely difficult to repeat such calculations for sets of interdependent projects. Now, it is possible to check a great number of project variants by permitting size, time-phasing, product mix, location, and technology to vary. Also, sets of interdependent projects can be analyzed more systematically. Given the complex and interdependent structure of most industrial sectors, these improvements in analytical techniques can be expected to have substantial impact on the quality of investment project and program design.

In this monograph, a model has been presented that is designed to enable the analyst to find quickly those investment projects or sets of investment projects which are the least expensive to implement, while meeting specified market requirements. The model includes final product shipments from plants to markets; intermediate product shipments among plants, exports, imports; choice of technology; investment cost characterized by economies of scale; and balance equations that link together raw materials, intermediate products, and final products. Furthermore, the model provides for the sale of by-products to other industries. These relationships constitute a linear mixed-integer programming model that can be used to search efficiently for the project variants or set of project variants that lead to the lowest cost.

The data requirements for the models presented in this volume are substantial. They are not so much dependent on the analytical approach to project planning, however, as on the issues it is desirable to address in that planning phase. The better the data base, the better the project planning that can be conducted; the critical tradeoff is not between data requirements and more or less simple project planning methods, but rather between good data together with good planning techniques and the cost of errors in investment project and program formulation. This is not to say that the approach to investment planning proposed in this volume is guaranteed not to lead to errors. By nature, investment decisions are made on the basis of predictions of the future, and the possibility of projection errors remains. Here the project selection model has two important advantages over more conventional methods of project planning. First, given a set of projections, the model is designed to identify a consistent investment program that is optimal, with some specification of the objective function. Second, the model permits rapid and efficient investigation of alternative investment program designs, even in the case of a set of interdependent activities. Most conventional methods of project planning do not provide this possibility, and, therefore, decisions need to be made on the basis of less knowledge about the structure of the planning problem at hand.

Despite all its advantages, the project planning model as it now stands has its limitations as well, and particular attention has been given to this aspect. The main purpose of that discussion is to make both the analyst and the users of the model aware of these limitations. It is hoped that this will prevent misuse of the method and give a clear indication of areas in which the methodology could be improved.

Finally, a discussion of solution methods has been provided. This is important because the speed of computers and algorithms limits the size of the combinatorial problems that can be solved. The popular image that a large computer can solve any problem within a few minutes needs correction. Rather, the computer can perform the calculations for many more variants than could a project analyst with a mechanical desk calculator, even though the number of variants is still limited. Therefore, it is important that the investment planning model be designed in such a way that the main focus is on the difficult choices, leaving the obvious choices out of the model framework. The project planning model can be used effectively only if from the start the investment planning exercise is conceived as one which requires the close cooperation of the analyst, the country and sector specialists, and the computer.

In summary, the model discussed in this volume offers the economic planner and engineer involved in project identification a method to address explicitly aspects of project planning that could not be handled conveniently before. Chief among these issues are time-phasing, scaling, location and technology of investments, and questions of product mix; moreover, the impact of interdependence among projects can be more systematically assessed. Although these issues have not been entirely disregarded to date, the efficiency of conventional project planning methods cannot compare with that provided by project planning models that are amenable to computerized solution procedures.

Index

Abramovitz, Moses, 12n

Bergendorff, Hans G., 13
Binary tree, 105–06
Branch and bound, 103, 105–10
By-products, 29, 50; in complete model, 51, 52

Capacity constraints, 19, 21, 37; in complete model, 53, 58, 60; data required about, 70–71; in multiproduct model, 27–28; in process model, 32; in transport model, 24
Capacity, excess, 3–4, 12, 115–21
Capacity utilization: coefficient for, 28; in complete model, 51, 53, 58, 60
Capital costs. See Investment cost
Capital recovery factor (CRF), 22, 40, 41, 47–49
Chenery, Hollis B., 12
Commodities: categories of, 30; in complete model, 51, 52–53, 57, 59–60; in multiproduct model, 27–29;

in process model, 31–32; set definition of, 30, 51; set specification and, 67; substitution and, 61, 98–99
Computer codes, 104–10
Consumer and producer surplus, 92–98
Cost. See Discounted costs; Investment cost; Production cost; Recurrent cost; Shadow prices; Transport cost
Cutoff point, 9–11

Dasgupta, Partha, 1n, 2n
Data requirements, 63–80; for demand, 67–69; discount rate and, 77; foreign exchange rate and, 77–78; for prices and costs, 72–77; set specification and, 63–67, 80; for supply, 69–72
Demand: data required about, 67–69; distribution of, 69; estimation of, 67–69; substitution and, 61, 98–99. See also Market requirements
Discounted costs, 45–49, 54

Discount rate, 77
Diseconomies of scale, investment cost function and, 43–44
Domestic markets, set definition and, 51
Duloy, John H., 92, 97

Economic intergration, 85–86
Economies of scale, 25; defined, 3; importance of, 111–14; investment cost function and, 38–43; as planning problem, 3–4; zero-one constraints and, 42–43
Enumeration, 105
Equations for the complete model, 52–55
Erlenkotter, Donald, 13
Excess capacity. *See* Capacity, excess
Export bounds. *See* Exports (limitations on)
Exports, 20–22; analysis of, 86–88; in complete model, 53–55; limitations on, 37, 61–62; set definition of, 51; set specification and, 65; specification of, 33–37

Final commodities. *See* Commodities
Foreign exchange rate, estimation of, 77–78
Frank, Charles, Jr., 13, 98

Gately, Dermot, 13
Geoffrion, Arthur M., 103n
Global optimum, 57, 107, 108
Goreux, Louis M., 120n

Haldi, John, 5
Hand calculations, 110–22; of augmented marginal costs, 118–20; of marginal cost and transport cost, 114–15; of marginal versus import costs, 11–14; of maximum plant scales, 115–18; of mutual exclusivity constraints, 120–22

Inman, Richard, 120n
Imports, 20–21; specification of, 33–37, 52–55
Input-output coefficients, 9, 30–32; data required about, 71–72
Integer constraints. *See* Zero-one constraints
Integration studies, 85–86
Interdependence, 1; importance of, 111–14
Intermediate commodities. *See* Commodities
Inventories, 16n
Investment cost, 21, 38; in complete model, 52, 53–54; defined, 38, 52; specification of, 38–45
Investment planning, 3–4

Judge, George G., 92

Kendrick, David A., 12, 13n, 101n
Knight, Frank H., 11, 12n

Labor, 45
LEGO. *See* Project selection model (LEGO set in)
Little, Ian M. D., 1n, 2n
Local optimum, 57, 108
Location. *See* Plant sites

Manne, Alan S., 12, 13, 118n, 120n
Marcus, Bruce T., 81n
Marglin, Stephen A., 1n, 2n
Market requirements, 17; in complete model, 53; with imports, 37; in

multiproduct model, 27, 29; in process model, 32–33; in transport model, 24

Markets: set definition of, 33, 51; set specification and, 65

Markowitz, Harry M., 12

Marsten, R. E., 103n

Material balances: in complete model, 52–53; with exports and imports, 36–37; with interplant shipments, 36–37; in multiproduct model, 28; in process model, 31–32

Meeraus, Alexander, 13, 98, 101n, 103n

Mirrlees, James A., 1n, 2n

Mixed-integer programming, 6–7, 57, 103–10

Model limitations, 90–102; fixed demands and, 91–98; fixed prices and, 99; size of computational problem and, 101; substitution and, 98–99; uncertainty and, 100

Model solution, 103–24; branch and bound in, 105–10; computer codes for, 104–11; hand calculations for, 110–22; marginal costs and, 111–15, 118–20; maximum plant scale and, 115–18, 120–21

Model use, 81–89; in export analysis, 86–88; integration studies and, 85–86; in project selection, 83–85; regulation and, 88–89; shipping patterns and, 82–83

Moore, Frederick T., 5n

Nationalization, determination of compensation and, 89

Node: defined, 105; hanging, 107

Norton, Roger D., 92, 97

Objective function, 9–11; in complete model, 54–55; in process model, 31; in transport model, 25, 26; value of, 107–10

Opportunity cost. *See* Shadow prices

Organization for Economic Cooperation and Development (OECD), 1, 2n

Overcapacity. *See* Capacity, excess

Parameters, symbol definitions for, 51–52

Plant scale: minimum efficient, 6; upper bound on, 42

Plant sites: set definition of, 33, 51; set specification and, 63–64

Policy objectives, 9, 100–01

Pratten, L. F., 5

Prices: data required about, 72–77; of exports and imports, 34; fixed, 99n; input, 31; regulation of, 88–89

Process, 19, 30; set definition of, 33, 51; set specification and, 66

Process model: described, 18–21; developed mathematically, 29–33; with international trade, 34–36; with interplant shipments, 33–38

Production cost, 17–18, defined, 26; specification of, 26, 27–28

Productive units, 18–22; defined, 28; set definition of, 33; set specification and, 68

Product substitution, 61, 98–99

Profit maximization, 97

Project evaluation, 1, 2

Project identification, 2

Project planning, 1, 4–9, 81–89; institutional restrictions on, 5; literature on, 11–14; rules of thumb for, 6; selection criterion for, 9–11; technical restrictions on, 5; under economies of scale, 6–9. *See also* Project selection model

Project selection model, 50–62; described, 21–22; export constraint in, 61, 62; final product substitution in, 61; indivisible investments and, 58; LEGO set in, 50, 61–62; mathematical structure of, 52–55; notation for, 51–52; size of, 55–57; size and time-phasing only in, 58–60; uses of, 83–85 (*see also* Project planning)

Raw materials. *See* Commodities
Recurrent cost, 20
Regulation, 88–89
Rhee, Yung Whee, 13, 113n
Rosenstein-Rodan, Paul N., 11, 12n

Samuelson, Paul A., 92
Sen, Amartya, 1n, 2n
Sets, defined, 51
Shadow prices, 2, 10
Shipments, 16–17; in complete model, 52–55; defined, 24; interplant, 19, 33–36; in multiproduct model, 28–29; specification of, 24–26; in transport model, 24
Shipping patterns, 82–83
Silberston, Aubrey, 5
Size of the complete model, 55–57; 101
Stoutjesdijk, Ardy J., 13, 98, 103n, 113n
Substitution. *See* Product substitution
Surplus. *See* Consumer and producer surplus

Takayama, Takashi, 92
Technology, 5, 6
Time periods: set definition of, 51; set specification and, 66–67
Transport cost: in complete model, 55; data required about, 77; defined, 25; specification of, 25–26; in transport model, 25
Transport model: described, 16–17; developed mathematically, 23–26; multiproduct, 27–29; with production cost, 17–18

Uncertainty, 100
Ungar, Arthur J., 81n
United Nations Industrial Development Organization (UNIDO), 1, 2

Variables, defined, 51
Vietorisz, Thomas, 12

Weigel, Dale, 13
Westphal, Larry E., 13, 98n, 103n, 113n
Whitcomb, Donald, 5
World Bank, 2

Young, Allyn, 11, 12n

Zero-one constraints, 42, 53